Don't Take Social Media Seriously

Shah Rukh

Published by Shah Rukh, 2024.

While every precaution has been taken in the preparation of this book, the publisher assumes no responsibility for errors or omissions, or for damages resulting from the use of the information contained herein.

DON'T TAKE SOCIAL MEDIA SERIOUSLY

First edition. June 18, 2024.

Copyright © 2024 Shah Rukh.

Written by Shah Rukh.

Table of Contents

Chapter 1: Introduction: The Social Media Illusion

Social media has become an integral part of modern life, fundamentally altering how we communicate, share information, and perceive the world around us. At its core, social media promises to connect us more closely with others, fostering community and providing a platform for self-expression. However, this ubiquitous presence in our lives comes with a complex and often overlooked underside, which can be described as the social media illusion. This concept encapsulates the misleading nature of social media, where the realities presented are often far removed from actual life experiences and emotions.

The allure of social media lies in its ability to create a seemingly perfect world. Platforms like Instagram, Facebook, Twitter, and TikTok allow users to curate their lives, presenting only the most attractive, exciting, and positive aspects. This carefully managed image can create a powerful illusion of perfection and success. Influencers, celebrities, and even our acquaintances often display snapshots of their lives that highlight achievements, beauty, wealth, and happiness. These images are meticulously selected and often enhanced with filters and editing tools to appear flawless. Consequently, this continuous exposure to idealized versions of life can lead to a distorted perception of reality.

One of the most profound impacts of this illusion is on self-esteem and mental health. When individuals constantly compare their lives to the polished and seemingly perfect lives displayed on social media, it can lead to feelings of inadequacy, envy, and dissatisfaction. This phenomenon is particularly pronounced among young people who are still developing their identities and self-worth. The pressure to conform to these idealized standards can result in anxiety, depression, and other mental health issues. Studies have shown that heavy social media use is correlated with increased rates of anxiety and depression, as well as negative body image and self-esteem.

Social media fosters a culture of validation and approval through likes, comments, and shares. These metrics become a measure of one's worth and popularity, driving users to seek constant affirmation from their online peers. This can create a cycle of dependency, where individuals feel compelled to post content that will garner positive feedback, reinforcing the illusion of a perfect life. The quest for online approval can become addictive, detracting from real-life interactions and experiences. It also perpetuates a superficial understanding of self-worth, tied to external validation rather than internal fulfillment.

The illusion of social media extends beyond individual self-perception to influence societal norms and values. It plays a significant role in shaping public opinion, cultural trends, and even political discourse. Social media platforms are designed to amplify content that generates engagement, often prioritizing sensational, controversial, or emotionally charged posts. This can distort public perception, creating echo chambers where individuals are exposed primarily to information that reinforces their existing beliefs. The spread of misinformation and fake news is a well-documented consequence of this dynamic, with serious implications for democracy and social cohesion.

The social media illusion has a profound impact on relationships. Online interactions can lack the depth and nuance of face-to-face communication, leading to superficial connections. The emphasis on image and presentation can also affect how individuals relate to each other, fostering jealousy, competition, and misunderstandings. In romantic relationships, social media can become a source of conflict, as partners may feel insecure or distrustful due to the curated interactions and connections displayed online. The pressure to maintain a perfect online persona can also strain friendships, as individuals may feel compelled to project an image that is not reflective of their true selves.

Another dimension of the social media illusion is the commodification of personal data. Social media platforms are primarily driven by advertising revenue, and user data is a valuable asset. The algorithms that power these platforms are designed to maximize user engagement, often at the expense of privacy and security. Users are encouraged to share more about their lives, preferences, and behaviors, which are then harvested and sold to advertisers. This exploitation of personal data raises significant ethical concerns and exposes users to risks such as data breaches, identity theft, and manipulation.

The labor behind maintaining an online presence is often invisible. Influencers and content creators invest significant time, effort, and resources into producing content that fits the idealized narrative. This labor is frequently underappreciated and can lead to burnout and stress. The pressure to constantly innovate and stay relevant in a fast-paced digital environment can be overwhelming. Despite the glamorous facade, the reality of sustaining a successful online persona is often far from idyllic.

The social media illusion also perpetuates unrealistic standards of beauty and success. The prevalence of edited and filtered images sets unattainable benchmarks for physical appearance and lifestyle. This can lead to a myriad of issues, including body dysmorphia, eating disorders, and an unhealthy obsession with material wealth. The constant barrage of images depicting luxurious lifestyles and physical perfection creates an environment where individuals feel perpetually inadequate, striving to meet standards that are not only unrealistic but also unhealthy.

The illusion of social media can obscure the socio-economic realities that underpin many of the images and narratives presented online. The apparent success and wealth displayed by influencers and celebrities often gloss over the privileges and opportunities that have enabled their success. This can create a misleading narrative that success is easily attainable through effort and charisma alone, ignoring the systemic barriers and inequalities that exist. For many, this illusion can foster unrealistic aspirations and a sense of failure when they are unable to replicate the success they see online.

The focus on visual and immediate gratification can undermine more substantial, long-term goals and values. The ephemeral nature of social media content encourages a culture of instant reward, where likes and shares provide immediate, yet fleeting, satisfaction. This can detract from pursuits that require sustained effort and delayed gratification, such as education, career development, and personal growth. The constant need for new content also fosters a disposable culture, where the value of information and experiences is diminished by their rapid consumption and replacement.

Chapter 2: The Birth of Social Media: A Brief History

The advent of social media represents a significant milestone in the evolution of communication and technology. Its origins trace back to the early days of the internet, evolving through various stages to become the complex and multifaceted ecosystem we experience today. Understanding the birth of social media involves exploring the technological advancements, cultural shifts, and entrepreneurial innovations that have shaped its development.

The seeds of social media were sown in the 1970s with the advent of the first recognizable social networking service, ARPANET (Advanced Research Projects Agency Network), a precursor to the internet. ARPANET was developed by the United States Department of Defense for research purposes, connecting several universities and research institutions. While not a social media platform by today's standards, ARPANET facilitated the sharing of information and laid the groundwork for online communication networks.

In the 1980s, the rise of Bulletin Board Systems (BBS) marked a significant step towards social networking. BBS allowed users to connect via dial-up modems, share files, and post messages on public forums. These systems were community-oriented, often localized, and they fostered the early development of online communities. BBS users could engage in discussions, share news, and even play games, creating a rudimentary form of social media interaction.

The 1990s witnessed the emergence of the World Wide Web, which revolutionized internet accessibility and set the stage for modern social media. One of the first social networking websites was Six Degrees, launched in 1997 by Andrew Weinreich. Named after the concept of "six degrees of separation," Six Degrees allowed users to create profiles, list their friends, and browse the friends' networks.

Although it was relatively short-lived, ceasing operations in 2001, Six Degrees is often credited as the first social media site that embodied many features of modern platforms.

The late 1990s and early 2000s saw the rise of other pioneering social networking sites. LiveJournal, launched in 1999, allowed users to create and share blog posts, forming online communities based on shared interests. Similarly, Friendster, launched in 2002, aimed to connect friends and acquaintances, but it struggled with technical issues and eventually declined in popularity. Despite its challenges, Friendster's early success highlighted the growing demand for online social networks.

LinkedIn, launched in 2003, took a different approach by focusing on professional networking. It allowed users to create professional profiles, connect with colleagues, and share career-related content. LinkedIn's emphasis on business and professional connections differentiated it from other social networking sites and established it as a valuable tool for job seekers and recruiters.

MySpace, launched in 2003, became a cultural phenomenon and played a pivotal role in popularizing social media. MySpace allowed users to create highly customizable profiles, share music, post blogs, and connect with friends. Its success was driven by its appeal to musicians and creative communities, who used the platform to share their work and connect with fans. At its peak, MySpace was the largest social networking site in the world, but it eventually declined due to competition and poor management decisions.

Facebook, launched in 2004 by Mark Zuckerberg and his college roommates, marked a significant turning point in the history of social media. Initially limited to Harvard students, Facebook quickly expanded to other universities and eventually opened to the general public. Its clean design, user-friendly interface, and emphasis on real-name identity set it apart from predecessors. Facebook introduced features such as the News Feed, which aggregated updates from friends and pages, fostering a more dynamic and engaging user experience. Over the years, Facebook has continuously evolved, adding new features such as photo sharing, messaging, and live streaming, solidifying its position as a dominant social media platform.

Twitter, launched in 2006, introduced a new paradigm in social networking with its focus on short, real-time messages called tweets. Twitter's 140-character limit (later expanded to 280 characters) encouraged concise communication and real-time updates, making it a popular platform for news, activism, and public discourse. Twitter's use of hashtags to categorize topics and facilitate searches became a defining feature, influencing the way information spreads on social media.

The rise of smartphones and mobile internet in the late 2000s and early 2010s further accelerated the growth of social media. Mobile apps allowed users to access social networks on the go, leading to increased engagement and the development of new platforms optimized for mobile use. Instagram, launched in 2010, capitalized on this trend by focusing on photo and video sharing through a mobile-first approach. Its simple interface and emphasis on visual content quickly attracted a large user base, and its acquisition by Facebook in 2012 further bolstered its growth.

Snapchat, launched in 2011, introduced the concept of ephemeral messaging, where photos and videos disappear after being viewed. This innovative approach to communication resonated with younger users and led to the development of features such as Stories, which allow users to share temporary content with their followers. Snapchat's success demonstrated the appeal of more casual and temporary forms of social interaction, influencing other platforms to adopt similar features.

The proliferation of social media platforms has continued into the 2010s and 2020s, with the emergence of new players such as TikTok. Launched internationally in 2018, TikTok focuses on short-form video content and has quickly become one of the most popular social media apps globally. Its algorithm-driven content discovery and emphasis on creativity and entertainment have made it particularly appealing to younger audiences, highlighting the ongoing evolution of social media trends.

Throughout its history, social media has been shaped by various technological, cultural, and economic factors. Advances in internet infrastructure, mobile technology, and software development have enabled the creation of increasingly sophisticated platforms. At the same time, cultural shifts towards digital communication and the desire for online social connections have driven user adoption and engagement. The commercialization of social media, through advertising and data monetization, has also played a crucial role in its development, influencing platform design and business strategies.

Chapter 3: Filters and Facades: The Unreal Reality

The phenomenon of filters and facades on social media has profoundly impacted how individuals present themselves and perceive others online. This unreal reality, constructed through carefully curated images, edited photos, and meticulously crafted narratives, creates a distorted version of life that can have far-reaching consequences on self-esteem, mental health, societal norms, and human relationships.

The use of filters and editing tools on social media platforms like Instagram, Snapchat, and TikTok has become ubiquitous. Filters are digital overlays that can enhance or alter photographs and videos, often to an almost unrecognizable degree. They can smooth skin, whiten teeth, alter facial features, and even change the scenery. While these tools can be fun and creative, allowing users to experiment with their appearance and environment, they also contribute to the creation of an idealized and often unattainable standard of beauty and lifestyle.

One of the most significant effects of filters is the promotion of unrealistic beauty standards. Filters can dramatically alter a person's appearance, making them look more conventionally attractive according to societal standards. For instance, many filters are designed to give users clearer skin, larger eyes, fuller lips, and slimmer faces. These alterations reinforce narrow definitions of beauty that are often based on Eurocentric features and youthfulness. As users repeatedly see these enhanced images, both from influencers and peers, they may begin to internalize these standards and feel pressure to conform to them. This can lead to a range of negative outcomes, including body dysmorphia, low self-esteem, and eating disorders.

The facade created by filters extends beyond individual photos to entire social media profiles. Users often curate their content to present an idealized version of their lives, showcasing moments of success, happiness, and beauty while omitting the more mundane or challenging aspects of their experiences. This selective sharing can create a misleading narrative that everyone else is living a perfect life, filled with constant excitement and joy. For those consuming this content, the comparison to their own less-than-perfect realities can be disheartening and lead to feelings of inadequacy and loneliness.

Influencers and celebrities play a significant role in perpetuating these facades. Many influencers build their brands around aspirational lifestyles, sharing images of luxurious vacations, high-end fashion, and impeccable homes. While some influencers are transparent about the use of filters and the effort that goes into creating their content, many are not, which can further blur the line between reality and fiction. The polished images and videos set an unattainable bar for ordinary users, who may not have the same resources or opportunities to curate their lives so meticulously. This disparity can foster a sense of failure and resentment among those who feel they cannot measure up.

The impact of filters and facades on mental health is profound. Studies have shown that exposure to heavily filtered images on social media can lead to increased anxiety, depression, and body image concerns. The constant comparison to others' idealized images can create a sense of perpetual inadequacy and dissatisfaction. For young people, who are still developing their sense of self and self-worth, the effects can be particularly damaging. Adolescents and young adults are highly susceptible to social comparison and are more likely to experience negative outcomes from exposure to unrealistic beauty standards and idealized lifestyles.

The use of filters and the creation of facades also affect interpersonal relationships. Online interactions can become superficial, focused more on appearances and perceptions than on genuine connections. People may feel compelled to present a certain image to gain approval and validation from their peers, leading to interactions that are based on performance rather than authenticity.

This can erode trust and intimacy in relationships, as individuals may hide their true selves behind carefully constructed online personas.

Moreover, the culture of filters and facades can lead to a lack of authenticity and vulnerability in online interactions. When everyone is trying to present a perfect image, there is little room for sharing struggles, failures, and imperfections. This can create an environment where individuals feel isolated in their challenges, believing that they are the only ones experiencing difficulties. The lack of honest and open communication can hinder meaningful connections and support networks, which are crucial for mental health and well-being.

The commodification of self-image is another significant aspect of the unreal reality created by filters and facades. Social media platforms are driven by algorithms that reward engagement, and attractive, polished images tend to garner more likes, comments, and shares. This creates an incentive for users to enhance their photos and curate their profiles meticulously to attract attention and gain followers. The pursuit of social media fame and validation can become all-consuming, leading individuals to invest significant time, effort, and even money into maintaining their online personas. This commodification of self-image can reduce individuals to mere products, valued primarily for their appearance and social media clout.

The societal implications of filters and facades are also noteworthy. The pervasive use of filters contributes to a culture that values superficiality and appearance over substance and authenticity. It reinforces the notion that one's worth is tied to their looks and their ability to project a desirable lifestyle. This can perpetuate harmful stereotypes and reinforce existing social inequalities, as those who do not conform to the idealized standards may be marginalized or discriminated against. The emphasis on visual perfection can overshadow more meaningful attributes, such as kindness, intelligence, and creativity.

Addressing the challenges posed by filters and facades requires a multifaceted approach. Increasing digital literacy is crucial, particularly for young people, to help them navigate the complexities of social media and develop a critical understanding of the content they consume. Educating users about the artificial nature of many images and the effort that goes into creating online personas can help mitigate the negative effects of comparison and unrealistic standards.

Promoting authenticity and transparency on social media platforms is also important. Influencers and celebrities can play a positive role by being open about the use of filters and the realities behind their curated images. Platforms themselves can implement features that encourage more authentic content, such as highlighting unedited photos or promoting mental health awareness. Additionally, there is a growing movement towards body positivity and self-acceptance, which seeks to challenge unrealistic beauty standards and celebrate diverse and authentic representations of beauty.

Ultimately, fostering a healthier relationship with social media involves balancing the desire for self-expression and creativity with the need for authenticity and genuine connection. While filters and curated images can be a fun and creative way to engage with social media, it is essential to remember that they often do not reflect the full reality of a person's life. By cultivating a more critical and mindful approach to social media use, individuals can better navigate the pressures of the unreal reality and build more meaningful and fulfilling online and offline lives.

Chapter 4: The Comparison Trap: Escaping the Endless Loop

The comparison trap is a pervasive issue exacerbated by the rise of social media, where individuals constantly measure their lives against the curated and often idealized lives of others. This endless loop of comparison can have detrimental effects on mental health, self-esteem, and overall well-being. Escaping the comparison trap requires a deep understanding of its roots, the mechanisms that sustain it, and practical strategies for fostering a healthier mindset and relationship with social media.

Social comparison is a natural human tendency. Psychologist Leon Festinger proposed the social comparison theory in 1954, suggesting that individuals have an inherent drive to evaluate themselves by comparing their abilities and opinions to those of others. This drive helps people understand where they stand in various aspects of life and can motivate self-improvement. However, the omnipresence of social media has magnified this tendency, creating an environment where comparison is constant and unavoidable.

On social media platforms like Instagram, Facebook, and TikTok, users are bombarded with images and stories of others' accomplishments, travels, relationships, and lifestyles. These platforms often emphasize the most glamorous and positive aspects of life, as users curate their content to showcase their best moments. This creates a skewed perception of reality, where it appears that everyone else is living a perfect, successful, and happy life. The highlight reels of others' lives become the benchmark against which individuals measure their own, often leading to feelings of inadequacy and dissatisfaction.

One of the primary mechanisms that sustain the comparison trap is the algorithm-driven nature of social media. Platforms are designed to maximize user engagement by showing content that generates strong emotional responses, often favoring posts that depict idealized and aspirational images. The more time users spend on the platform, the more they are exposed to these curated lives, perpetuating the cycle of comparison. The algorithms prioritize content that is likely to receive likes, comments, and shares, which typically includes posts that align with societal standards of beauty, success, and happiness.

The impact of this constant comparison is profound, particularly on mental health. Research has shown that heavy social media use is associated with increased levels of anxiety, depression, and loneliness. When individuals compare their real, often messy lives with the polished versions they see online, they may feel that they are falling short in various aspects, such as their appearance, career achievements, or social lives. This can lead to a negative self-image and lower self-esteem, as individuals internalize the belief that they are not good enough.

The comparison trap is especially harmful to adolescents and young adults, who are in a critical phase of developing their identities and self-worth. Young people are particularly vulnerable to social comparison, as they seek validation and approval from their peers. The pressure to conform to the idealized standards presented on social media can lead to a range of negative outcomes, including body dissatisfaction, eating disorders, and a preoccupation with appearance. The pursuit of social media validation through likes and followers can also become addictive, detracting from more meaningful activities and relationships.

Escaping the endless loop of comparison requires intentional effort and a shift in mindset. The first step in escaping the comparison trap is to recognize when and how it occurs. Mindfulness practices can help individuals become more aware of their thoughts and emotions when using social media. By identifying triggers and patterns of comparison, individuals can begin to challenge and reframe their automatic responses. Reducing the amount of time spent on social media can decrease exposure to comparison-inducing content. Setting boundaries, such as designated social media-free times or limiting daily usage, can help individuals regain control over their social media habits. Using apps that track and limit screen time can also be beneficial. Taking control of the content that appears in one's social media feed can mitigate the effects of the comparison trap. Unfollowing or muting accounts that consistently evoke negative feelings and following those that promote positivity, authenticity, and self-acceptance can create a healthier online environment. Diversifying the types of content consumed, including educational, inspirational, and humorous posts, can also reduce the focus on appearance and lifestyle comparisons.

Practicing gratitude can shift the focus from what is lacking to what is present and appreciated in one's life. Keeping a gratitude journal or regularly reflecting on positive aspects of one's life can counteract the negative effects of social comparison. Gratitude can foster a sense of contentment and satisfaction, reducing the need to compare oneself to others. Self-compassion involves treating oneself with the same kindness and understanding that one would offer to a friend. It encourages individuals to recognize that everyone has flaws and struggles, and that self-worth is not contingent on external achievements or appearances. Practicing self-compassion can help individuals become more resilient to the negative effects of social comparison.

Pursuing activities that align with one's values and interests can provide a sense of fulfillment and purpose, reducing the reliance on social media for validation. Engaging in hobbies, volunteering, and spending time with loved ones can create meaningful connections and experiences that enhance well-being. Building and nurturing genuine relationships can provide a sense of belonging and support that is often lacking in superficial online interactions. Face-to-face communication and meaningful conversations can foster deeper connections and reduce the emphasis on social media as a primary source of social interaction.

Questioning and critically analyzing the standards of beauty and success presented on social media can help individuals develop a more realistic and balanced perspective. Recognizing that many images are edited, filtered, and selectively shared can diminish their impact. Advocating for and supporting body positivity and diversity can also contribute to a broader acceptance of different appearances and lifestyles. For those struggling with the severe effects of social comparison, seeking professional help from a therapist or counselor can be beneficial. Mental health professionals can provide guidance and support in developing healthier coping strategies and addressing underlying issues related to self-esteem and body image.

Using social media in a way that aligns with one's values and goals can transform it into a positive tool rather than a source of stress. Sharing authentic content, supporting others, and engaging in constructive discussions can create a more uplifting and supportive online community. The comparison trap is a pervasive issue exacerbated by social media, where individuals constantly measure their lives against idealized versions of others' lives. This endless loop of comparison can have detrimental effects on mental health, self-esteem, and overall well-being. Escaping the comparison trap requires awareness, intentional effort, and a shift in mindset. By limiting social media use, curating one's feed, practicing gratitude and self-compassion, engaging in meaningful activities, and seeking authentic connections, individuals can foster a healthier relationship with social media and reduce the negative impact of comparison. Challenging unrealistic standards and promoting positive use of social media can further contribute to a more balanced and fulfilling life. Through these strategies, individuals can break free from the cycle of comparison and cultivate a sense of contentment and self-worth that is grounded in their unique experiences and values.

Chapter 5: Influencer Culture: Behind the Scenes

Influencer culture has emerged as a dominant force in the realm of social media, transforming ordinary individuals into powerful figures capable of shaping public opinion, driving consumer behavior, and creating trends. Behind the scenes of this seemingly glamorous world lies a complex and multifaceted landscape characterized by strategic planning, relentless effort, personal sacrifices, and the ever-present pressure to maintain relevance and authenticity.

At its core, influencer culture revolves around individuals who have amassed large followings on social media platforms such as Instagram, YouTube, TikTok, and Twitter. These influencers wield significant influence over their audiences, often becoming trusted sources of information, entertainment, and inspiration. The journey to becoming an influencer typically begins with a passion for a particular niche—be it fashion, beauty, fitness, travel, or lifestyle. However, transitioning from a casual content creator to a full-fledged influencer requires a strategic and calculated approach.

One of the critical components behind the scenes of influencer culture is content creation. Influencers invest substantial time and effort into producing high-quality content that resonates with their audience. This process involves meticulous planning, from conceptualizing ideas to executing them flawlessly. Influencers must stay attuned to current trends and audience preferences, constantly adapting their content to remain relevant. This often means keeping up with platform algorithms, understanding what type of content is being favored, and adjusting their strategies accordingly.

The actual creation of content can be an arduous task. For a single Instagram post, influencers may spend hours setting up the perfect shot, editing the image, and crafting an engaging caption. On YouTube, creating a video involves scripting, filming, editing, and often multiple rounds of revisions. TikTok influencers might need to perfect a dance routine or comedic skit through numerous takes before achieving the desired result. The behind-the-scenes reality is that what appears as effortless and spontaneous on social media often requires extensive preparation and production.

Another crucial aspect of influencer culture is the building and maintaining of an online persona. Influencers curate their online presence carefully to create a brand that is both appealing and relatable to their followers. This involves making deliberate choices about the types of content they share, the tone of their messages, and the overall aesthetic of their profiles. While some influencers opt for a polished and aspirational image, others may choose a more raw and authentic approach. Regardless of the style, the goal is to cultivate a persona that resonates with the audience and fosters a sense of connection and trust.

Monetization is a significant driving force behind influencer culture. Influencers can earn income through various streams, including sponsored posts, brand collaborations, affiliate marketing, merchandise sales, and ad revenue. Sponsored posts and brand collaborations are particularly lucrative, as companies are willing to pay substantial sums for influencers to promote their products or services. However, these partnerships require careful negotiation and management to ensure alignment between the influencer's brand and the company's values. Influencers must also navigate the fine line between authentic promotion and blatant advertising to maintain their credibility with their audience.

The pursuit of monetization brings with it a host of challenges. Influencers often face pressure to consistently deliver engaging content to meet the demands of their followers and sponsors. This can lead to burnout, as the relentless need to produce content leaves little room for breaks or downtime. Additionally, the competition within the influencer space is fierce, with new creators emerging constantly. To stay ahead, influencers must continually innovate and find ways to differentiate themselves from others in their niche.

The pressure to maintain authenticity while monetizing their influence is a delicate balancing act. Followers are quick to detect inauthenticity, and overly commercial content can erode trust and loyalty. Influencers must be selective about the brands they partner with, ensuring that collaborations align with their personal values and resonate with their audience. This often involves turning down lucrative deals that do not fit their brand, which can be a difficult decision given the financial implications.

Behind the scenes, influencers also grapple with the psychological toll of their public personas. The constant scrutiny and judgment from followers can take a significant emotional toll. Negative comments, criticism, and online harassment are common experiences for many influencers. The pressure to maintain a flawless image can lead to feelings of inadequacy and anxiety. Moreover, the blurring of boundaries between personal and public life can create a sense of isolation, as influencers navigate the complexities of sharing intimate aspects of their lives with a vast audience while maintaining some degree of privacy.

The personal sacrifices made by influencers are often overlooked. The time and effort required to build and sustain an influential online presence can strain personal relationships and limit time spent on other pursuits. Many influencers find themselves constantly connected to their devices, managing their online presence and engaging with their followers. This can lead to a work-life imbalance, where the lines between personal time and professional responsibilities are perpetually blurred.

In addition to personal sacrifices, influencers must also stay vigilant about the ethical implications of their influence. The responsibility of wielding significant power over public opinion and consumer behavior is immense. Influencers have a duty to promote ethical practices, avoid spreading misinformation, and use their platforms for positive impact. This involves being transparent about sponsored content, promoting products they genuinely believe in, and using their influence to raise awareness about important social issues.

Despite the challenges, influencer culture also offers numerous rewards. Successful influencers enjoy financial independence, creative freedom, and the opportunity to impact the lives of their followers positively. Many influencers use their platforms to advocate for causes they are passionate about, effecting real change and raising awareness about critical issues. The sense of community and connection with followers can also be deeply fulfilling, as influencers build supportive and engaged communities around their content.

The behind-the-scenes reality of influencer culture also highlights the importance of collaboration and support within the influencer community. Influencers often network with one another, share insights and strategies, and collaborate on projects to expand their reach and influence. These collaborations can be mutually beneficial, providing opportunities for cross-promotion and the sharing of diverse perspectives.

The evolving landscape of social media continues to shape the influencer culture. Emerging platforms, changing algorithms, and shifting audience preferences require influencers to stay adaptable and innovative. The rise of micro-influencers—individuals with smaller but highly engaged followings—demonstrates the increasing value of authenticity and niche expertise. Brands are recognizing the power of micro-influencers to connect with specific audiences in meaningful ways, leading to a more diversified and inclusive influencer ecosystem.

Chapter 6: The Metrics Myth: Followers, Likes, and Validation

The advent of social media has transformed how individuals perceive success, popularity, and self-worth, creating an environment where followers, likes, and other metrics are often seen as the ultimate validation. The allure of these metrics, however, is a double-edged sword. While they can provide a sense of accomplishment and recognition, they also perpetuate a myth that equates numerical popularity with personal value and success. This "metrics myth" has far-reaching implications on individuals' mental health, societal interactions, and the authenticity of online engagement.

The metrics myth is deeply rooted in the design and function of social media platforms. These platforms are engineered to maximize user engagement, and one of the most effective ways to achieve this is through the use of quantifiable feedback mechanisms. Likes, comments, shares, and follower counts are prominently displayed, providing immediate and tangible indicators of social approval. These metrics serve as a form of social currency, where higher numbers are often equated with greater social influence, attractiveness, and success.

The psychological impact of these metrics cannot be understated. Humans are inherently social creatures, driven by a need for acceptance and validation from their peers. Social media exploits this need by providing a constant stream of feedback. Each like, follow, or positive comment triggers a release of dopamine, the brain's reward chemical, creating a pleasurable sensation that encourages repeated behavior. This cycle can quickly become addictive, as users seek to replicate the positive feelings associated with social approval.

However, the metrics myth fosters an environment where quantity often trumps quality. The emphasis on numerical popularity encourages users to prioritize content that is likely to garner the most engagement, rather than content that is genuinely meaningful or authentic. This can lead to a homogenization of social media, where trending topics, viral challenges, and sensationalized content dominate feeds, overshadowing more nuanced or substantive discussions. The pursuit of likes and followers can also drive individuals to conform to perceived standards of beauty, lifestyle, and behavior, stifling diversity and individuality.

The pressure to achieve high engagement can have significant mental health implications. Studies have shown that heavy social media use is associated with increased rates of anxiety, depression, and low self-esteem. When individuals measure their worth based on social media metrics, they are more likely to experience feelings of inadequacy and dissatisfaction. This is particularly pronounced among adolescents and young adults, who are in a critical stage of identity formation and are highly sensitive to social comparison. The constant exposure to idealized images and curated lives can create unrealistic expectations, leading to body image issues, FOMO (fear of missing out), and a perpetual sense of not measuring up.

The metrics myth also impacts interpersonal relationships. The emphasis on public validation can shift the focus from genuine connections to superficial interactions. People may prioritize maintaining a polished online persona over fostering deep, meaningful relationships. This can result in a paradox where individuals are more connected than ever digitally, yet feel increasingly isolated and lonely. The pressure to present a perfect life online can also strain personal relationships, as the line between public and private life becomes blurred.

The commercial aspect of social media further complicates the metrics myth. Brands and advertisers recognize the power of influencers—individuals with large followings and high engagement rates—to drive consumer behavior. This has led to the monetization of social media metrics, where influencers are compensated based on their ability to attract and engage audiences. While this can provide lucrative opportunities for content creators, it also reinforces the idea that follower counts and likes are measures of success. The commodification of social media metrics can incentivize dishonest practices, such as purchasing followers or using engagement bots, to inflate numbers and appear more influential than one truly is.

The metrics myth extends beyond individual users and influencers to organizations, celebrities, and even politicians, who also seek to leverage social media for visibility and influence. The pursuit of high engagement can lead to a prioritization of sensationalism and controversy over accuracy and integrity. This is particularly concerning in the context of news and information dissemination, where the spread of misinformation and fake news can be amplified by the desire for clicks, shares, and likes.

Addressing the pervasive influence of the metrics myth requires a multifaceted approach. One of the most effective strategies is to cultivate digital literacy and critical thinking skills among social media users. By understanding the algorithms and psychological mechanisms that drive social media engagement, individuals can become more mindful of their online behaviors and less susceptible to the allure of metrics. Educating users about the potential harms of excessive social media use and promoting healthier digital habits can also mitigate the negative impacts on mental health.

Platforms themselves have a role to play in de-emphasizing metrics as the primary measure of value. This could involve redesigning interfaces to prioritize meaningful interactions over numerical popularity. For example, some platforms have experimented with hiding like counts or follower numbers to reduce social comparison and pressure. Encouraging diverse and authentic content through algorithmic adjustments and providing tools for users to manage their engagement more effectively can also contribute to a healthier online environment.

On a societal level, challenging the metrics myth involves redefining success and value in broader terms. Recognizing and celebrating achievements, creativity, and contributions that are not necessarily reflected in social media metrics can shift the focus from quantity to quality. This includes valuing offline interactions, personal growth, and community involvement. Promoting narratives that emphasize the importance of authenticity, vulnerability, and diversity can also counteract the homogenizing effects of the metrics myth.

Mental health support is crucial for those struggling with the pressures of social media validation. Providing access to counseling, support groups, and resources can help individuals navigate the challenges of the digital age. Encouraging open conversations about the realities of social media, including its potential harms and the importance of self-care, can reduce stigma and promote mental well-being.

Finally, influencers and content creators themselves can play a significant role in debunking the metrics myth. By sharing their own experiences with the pressures and challenges of social media, they can provide a more nuanced and realistic perspective for their followers. Embracing authenticity, vulnerability, and transparency in their content can foster a more supportive and understanding online community. Highlighting the importance of mental health, self-worth, and genuine connections over numerical popularity can set a positive example and inspire others to do the same.

Chapter 7: Digital Detox: Reclaiming Your Time

In the contemporary digital age, where smartphones and social media platforms dominate daily life, the concept of a digital detox has gained prominence as a vital practice for reclaiming one's time and well-being. A digital detox involves intentionally reducing or eliminating the use of digital devices and online services to restore balance, improve mental health, and foster real-world connections.

The need for a digital detox arises from the pervasive influence of technology on modern life. Smartphones, tablets, and computers have become indispensable tools for communication, work, entertainment, and information access. While these devices offer numerous advantages, their overuse can lead to negative consequences. Studies have shown that excessive screen time is associated with increased levels of stress, anxiety, and depression. The constant barrage of notifications, messages, and updates can create a sense of urgency and pressure, making it difficult to relax and unwind. Moreover, the allure of social media platforms, with their endless scroll and curated content, can lead to addictive behaviors and a distorted perception of reality.

One of the primary benefits of a digital detox is the improvement of mental health. Reducing screen time can alleviate symptoms of anxiety and depression by decreasing exposure to negative and stressful content. The constant comparison to others' idealized lives on social media can erode self-esteem and contribute to feelings of inadequacy. By stepping away from these platforms, individuals can cultivate a more positive self-image and focus on their own achievements and well-being. Additionally, a digital detox can enhance mindfulness and presence, allowing individuals to engage fully in the present moment without the distraction of digital devices.

Reclaiming time is another significant advantage of a digital detox. The average person spends several hours each day on their smartphone, often engaging in activities that are not particularly productive or fulfilling. By reducing or eliminating this time, individuals can redirect their energy towards more meaningful pursuits. This might include hobbies, physical exercise, reading, or spending quality time with loved ones. The regained time can also be used for personal growth and development, such as learning new skills, pursuing educational opportunities, or engaging in creative projects.

A successful digital detox requires careful planning and a commitment to making lasting changes in one's digital habits. The first step is to set clear and realistic goals. This might involve identifying specific times of day to be device-free, such as during meals, before bed, or during certain hours of the weekend. Setting boundaries around technology use can create a structured approach to reducing screen time. For example, establishing a rule of no phones in the bedroom can promote better sleep hygiene and a more restful night's sleep.

Creating a conducive environment for a digital detox is also crucial. This might involve designating certain areas of the home as tech-free zones, such as the dining room or the living room. Removing or hiding apps that are particularly addictive can reduce temptation and make it easier to stick to detox goals. Using tools and apps designed to limit screen time, such as those that track usage or block access to certain websites during specified hours, can also be beneficial.

Engaging in alternative activities is essential for a successful digital detox. Finding hobbies and interests that do not involve screens can provide a fulfilling way to spend reclaimed time. Physical activities, such as hiking, yoga, or team sports, offer both physical and mental health benefits. Creative pursuits, such as painting, writing, or playing a musical instrument, can provide a sense of accomplishment and satisfaction. Social activities, such as spending time with friends and family, can strengthen relationships and create lasting memories.

Mindfulness practices can complement a digital detox by promoting presence and awareness. Techniques such as meditation, deep breathing exercises, and journaling can help individuals tune into their thoughts and emotions, reducing the impulse to reach for digital devices as a distraction. Practicing gratitude and focusing on positive experiences can shift attention away from the digital world and towards the richness of real-life experiences.

While the benefits of a digital detox are clear, individuals may face several challenges in implementing and maintaining this practice. One common obstacle is the pervasive nature of technology in daily life. Many people rely on digital devices for work, communication, and information, making it difficult to fully disconnect. To address this, individuals can adopt a gradual approach to detox, starting with small, manageable steps and gradually increasing the duration and intensity of device-free periods.

Social pressure and FOMO (fear of missing out) can also hinder a digital detox. The desire to stay connected and up-to-date with friends, family, and current events can make it challenging to step away from social media and other online platforms. To mitigate this, individuals can communicate their detox plans to their social circles, explaining the importance of this practice for their well-being. Finding offline ways to stay connected, such as phone calls or in-person meetings, can maintain social bonds without relying on digital devices.

Another challenge is the potential for boredom and restlessness during a digital detox. Many people use their devices as a way to fill idle time and avoid boredom. To counter this, individuals can prepare a list of activities and projects to engage in during their detox. Having a variety of options available can prevent feelings of restlessness and provide a sense of purpose and direction.

The workplace presents its own set of challenges for a digital detox. Many jobs require constant connectivity and access to digital devices. In such cases, individuals can focus on setting boundaries around non-essential screen time. This might include turning off notifications for non-work-related apps, taking regular breaks from screens, and setting specific times for checking emails and messages. Communicating with employers and colleagues about the intention to reduce screen time can also foster a supportive work environment.

Despite these challenges, the rewards of a digital detox make it a worthwhile endeavor. By reclaiming time and reducing reliance on digital devices, individuals can experience a range of benefits, including improved mental health, enhanced relationships, and greater overall well-being. The process of detoxing from digital devices can also foster a deeper understanding of one's habits and triggers, leading to more intentional and mindful technology use in the future.

Chapter 8: The Echo Chamber Effect: Breaking Free from Bias

The Echo Chamber Effect is a phenomenon that occurs when individuals are exposed only to information, opinions, and beliefs that align with their own, leading to a reinforcement and amplification of their existing viewpoints. This effect is particularly pronounced on social media platforms, where algorithms curate content based on user preferences, engagement history, and social connections. These platforms create personalized newsfeeds, presenting information that aligns with users' previous interactions, thereby fostering environments where diverse perspectives are rare and confirmation bias flourishes.

Social media algorithms are designed to maximize user engagement. To achieve this, they prioritize content that users are more likely to interact with, such as posts from friends, liked pages, and previously engaged topics. This personalization leads to a filtering process that selectively presents information aligning with users' beliefs, effectively creating a self-reinforcing feedback loop. As a result, users are consistently exposed to content that confirms their existing views while dissenting opinions and contradictory information are filtered out or significantly underrepresented.

One of the primary dangers of the echo chamber effect is the entrenchment of pre-existing biases. When individuals are only exposed to information that supports their beliefs, they become more confident in the accuracy and universality of their perspectives. This reinforcement can lead to the radicalization of views, as the continuous affirmation from like-minded peers and sources emboldens individuals to adopt more extreme positions. Over time, this can foster a divisive and polarized environment, where constructive dialogue becomes increasingly difficult, and societal fragmentation intensifies.

The echo chamber effect also has significant implications for misinformation and the spread of false information. Within an echo chamber, false information can proliferate rapidly because it is less likely to be challenged or corrected. When users are consistently exposed to unverified or misleading content that aligns with their beliefs, they are more inclined to accept it as true. The lack of diverse viewpoints and critical scrutiny within echo chambers allows misinformation to gain credibility and spread unchecked, contributing to the broader problem of fake news.

Breaking free from the echo chamber effect requires conscious effort and deliberate actions. One effective approach is actively seeking out diverse perspectives and challenging one's own beliefs. This can be done by following a variety of news sources, engaging with people who have different viewpoints, and participating in discussions with an open mind. By exposing oneself to a broader range of information and opinions, individuals can gain a more balanced understanding of complex issues and reduce the risk of becoming entrenched in biased thinking.

Social media platforms also have a role to play in mitigating the echo chamber effect. While their primary goal is to enhance user engagement, they can implement features and policies that promote exposure to diverse viewpoints. For instance, platforms could adjust their algorithms to include a wider variety of content in users' feeds, regardless of prior engagement patterns. They could also highlight fact-checked articles and provide context for controversial or widely disputed claims. Additionally, encouraging respectful dialogue and creating spaces for civil discourse can help counteract the divisive tendencies fostered by echo chambers.

Educational initiatives can also be instrumental in combating the echo chamber effect. Teaching media literacy and critical thinking skills from an early age can equip individuals with the tools to critically evaluate information and recognize biases in their own thinking.

Educational programs can emphasize the importance of seeking out multiple sources of information, understanding the motivations behind content creation, and questioning the reliability and credibility of sources. By fostering a culture of critical inquiry, society can become more resilient to the distorting influences of echo chambers.

The echo chamber effect is not a new phenomenon, but social media has amplified its impact to unprecedented levels. In the past, people were more likely to be exposed to diverse viewpoints through traditional media, community interactions, and public discourse. However, the personalized nature of social media has intensified the insularity of information bubbles. To address this, individuals, platforms, and society as a whole must work together to promote information diversity, critical thinking, and respectful dialogue.

Chapter 9: FOMO: The Fear of Missing Out Explained

The Fear of Missing Out, commonly referred to as FOMO, is a pervasive psychological phenomenon that has become increasingly prevalent in the age of social media. FOMO is characterized by the anxiety that others might be having rewarding experiences from which one is absent. This feeling is exacerbated by the constant barrage of social media updates showcasing friends, celebrities, and acquaintances engaging in seemingly enviable activities. FOMO can manifest as a persistent concern that one is missing out on social events, opportunities, and life experiences, leading to feelings of inadequacy, restlessness, and discontent.

At its core, FOMO is driven by the human need for social connection and belonging. Humans are inherently social creatures, and being part of a community or group is fundamental to our psychological well-being. Social media platforms, with their curated feeds and highlight reels, present a skewed representation of reality, often emphasizing the positive and glamorous aspects of life while omitting the mundane or challenging moments. This selective sharing creates an illusion that everyone else is leading a more fulfilling, exciting, and successful life, triggering FOMO in those who perceive themselves as missing out.

The impact of FOMO on mental health can be profound. Individuals experiencing FOMO may suffer from increased levels of anxiety, depression, and loneliness. The constant comparison with others can erode self-esteem and lead to feelings of inadequacy. When people see their peers engaging in activities they deem desirable, they may feel a sense of regret or dissatisfaction with their own lives. This can create a vicious cycle, where the more individuals compare themselves to others, the worse they feel, prompting even more social media use in an attempt to feel connected and informed.

One of the key factors contributing to FOMO is the ubiquitous nature of smartphones and the internet. With the ability to access social media platforms at any time and from any location, people are constantly bombarded with updates about what others are doing. This perpetual connectivity means that there is no respite from the potential triggers of FOMO. Even when engaging in enjoyable activities, individuals might still feel the urge to check their phones, fearing they might miss out on something important or exciting happening elsewhere.

FOMO is not limited to social events or activities; it can also extend to material possessions, career opportunities, and personal achievements. For example, seeing friends purchase new gadgets, travel to exotic destinations, or receive promotions can induce feelings of envy and a fear of being left behind. This can lead to a relentless pursuit of more – more experiences, more possessions, more success – in an attempt to keep up with perceived social standards. However, this chase for constant gratification often leaves individuals feeling more exhausted and unfulfilled.

Social media influencers and marketers exploit FOMO to drive engagement and sales. By showcasing exclusive events, limited-time offers, and aspirational lifestyles, they create a sense of urgency and desirability. The fear of missing out on these exclusive opportunities can compel individuals to make impulsive decisions, such as purchasing products they do not need or attending events solely to be part of the experience. This exploitation of FOMO can have financial consequences, as people spend money on things that do not necessarily contribute to their long-term happiness or well-being.

Combating FOMO requires a multifaceted approach. One of the most effective strategies is practicing mindfulness and gratitude. By focusing on the present moment and appreciating what one has, individuals can reduce the tendency to compare themselves to others. Mindfulness exercises, such as meditation and deep breathing, can help calm the mind and diminish the constant urge to check social media. Keeping a gratitude journal, where one regularly notes things they are thankful for, can shift focus from what is lacking to what is abundant in one's life.

Another important step in addressing FOMO is curating one's social media environment. Unfollowing or muting accounts that trigger negative emotions can create a healthier online experience. Following accounts that inspire positivity, self-improvement, and authenticity can contribute to a more balanced perspective. Additionally, setting boundaries for social media use, such as designated times for checking updates or implementing screen-free periods, can help mitigate the incessant pull of online engagement.

Engaging in real-world activities and nurturing offline relationships can also counteract FOMO. Spending quality time with family and friends, pursuing hobbies, and participating in community events can provide a sense of fulfillment and connection that digital interactions often lack. These real-world experiences can serve as a reminder that life's richness is not solely defined by what is seen on social media.

Education about the nature of social media can further empower individuals to combat FOMO. Understanding that social media often presents an idealized version of reality can help people recognize that they are only seeing a small, curated part of others' lives. This awareness can reduce the impact of comparisons and help individuals develop a more realistic and compassionate view of themselves and their circumstances.

In the workplace, promoting a culture that values well-being over constant connectivity can alleviate FOMO-related stress. Encouraging employees to take breaks, disconnect after work hours, and engage in activities that promote work-life balance can enhance overall satisfaction and productivity. Organizations can also provide resources and support for mental health, fostering an environment where employees feel valued and connected without the pressure to always be "on."

Chapter 10: Mental Health and Social Media: Finding Balance

The relationship between mental health and social media is complex and multifaceted, often characterized by both positive and negative effects. In the digital age, social media platforms have become integral to daily life, offering unprecedented opportunities for communication, community building, and information sharing. However, the pervasive use of these platforms also presents significant challenges to mental health, necessitating a careful consideration of how to find balance and mitigate potential harms.

Social media can have numerous positive effects on mental health. For many people, these platforms provide a crucial means of staying connected with friends and family, especially those who live far away. Social media allows individuals to maintain relationships and build new connections, fostering a sense of community and belonging. For those who might feel isolated or marginalized in their offline lives, online communities can offer support and validation. For example, individuals dealing with specific health issues, mental illnesses, or personal challenges can find support groups and networks that provide empathy, advice, and shared experiences, which can be incredibly therapeutic.

Furthermore, social media can serve as a powerful tool for self-expression and creativity. Platforms like Instagram, TikTok, and YouTube allow users to share their talents, ideas, and personal stories with a global audience. This can enhance self-esteem and provide a sense of accomplishment. Additionally, the vast amount of information available on social media can be a valuable resource for learning and personal development. Users can access educational content, stay informed about current events, and engage in meaningful discussions on a wide range of topics.

However, despite these benefits, the negative impacts of social media on mental health are well-documented and can be severe. One of the primary concerns is the effect of social media on self-esteem and body image. The constant exposure to curated images and highlights of others' lives can lead to unrealistic comparisons and feelings of inadequacy. This is particularly pronounced among young people, who are more vulnerable to peer pressure and the influence of social norms. Studies have shown that excessive social media use can contribute to body dissatisfaction, anxiety, and depression, as users compare themselves unfavorably to the idealized representations they see online.

Another significant issue is the phenomenon of cyberbullying, which can have devastating effects on mental health. Unlike traditional forms of bullying, cyberbullying can occur around the clock and reach a wide audience quickly. Victims of cyberbullying often experience increased levels of anxiety, depression, and suicidal ideation. The anonymity provided by the internet can embolden individuals to engage in aggressive or harmful behaviors that they might not exhibit in face-to-face interactions.

The addictive nature of social media is another major concern. Platforms are designed to maximize user engagement through features such as notifications, likes, and endless scrolling. This design can lead to compulsive use, where individuals feel the need to check their accounts frequently, often at the expense of other activities. This can result in decreased productivity, disrupted sleep patterns, and increased stress levels. The constant influx of information and the pressure to stay updated can also lead to information overload, further exacerbating feelings of stress and anxiety.

To find a balance between the benefits and drawbacks of social media use, it is essential to develop strategies that promote healthy usage patterns and mitigate negative impacts. One effective approach is to set clear boundaries and limits on social media use. This can include designated times for checking social media, setting time limits on usage, and creating tech-free zones or periods, such as during meals or before bed. By establishing these boundaries, individuals can reduce the risk of compulsive use and create more time for offline activities that promote well-being.

Mindfulness practices can also play a crucial role in finding balance. Being mindful of one's social media use involves paying attention to how time spent online affects one's mood and mental state. Individuals can practice mindful engagement by taking regular breaks, being intentional about the content they consume, and avoiding mindless scrolling. Additionally, mindfulness techniques such as meditation and deep breathing can help individuals manage stress and anxiety related to social media use.

Curating one's social media environment is another important strategy. This involves being selective about the accounts one follows and the content one engages with. Following accounts that promote positivity, inspiration, and educational content can enhance the online experience, while unfollowing or muting accounts that trigger negative emotions can reduce stress and anxiety. Engaging with diverse perspectives and content can also provide a more balanced view of the world, counteracting the echo chamber effect.

Education and awareness are key to promoting healthy social media use. By understanding the potential impacts of social media on mental health, individuals can make more informed choices about their online behavior. Schools, parents, and organizations can play a significant role in educating young people about responsible social media use, cyberbullying prevention, and the importance of offline activities for mental health. Providing resources and support for those struggling with the negative effects of social media can also help mitigate its impact.

Social media platforms themselves have a responsibility to create environments that support mental health. This can include implementing features that promote digital well-being, such as usage tracking tools, reminders to take breaks, and options to filter or limit content. Platforms can also take a more active role in combating cyberbullying and misinformation by enforcing community guidelines and providing support for victims. Collaborating with mental health organizations to develop resources and campaigns that promote healthy social media use can further enhance these efforts.

In the workplace, fostering a culture that values work-life balance and digital well-being can help employees manage the impact of social media. Encouraging employees to disconnect during non-work hours, providing access to mental health resources, and promoting offline activities can enhance overall well-being. Organizations can also lead by example by implementing policies that reduce digital overload and support mental health.

Chapter 11: Cyberbullying: The Dark Side of Connectivity

Cyberbullying represents a significant and distressing aspect of modern connectivity, posing severe challenges to mental health, safety, and well-being, particularly among young people. This phenomenon involves the use of digital platforms such as social media, messaging apps, and online forums to harass, intimidate, or demean individuals. Unlike traditional forms of bullying, cyberbullying can occur around the clock, reach a vast audience almost instantly, and be conducted anonymously, making it exceptionally pervasive and harmful.

The nature of cyberbullying encompasses a wide range of behaviors, including spreading rumors, posting derogatory comments, sharing private information without consent, and sending threatening messages. These actions can have devastating effects on the victims, often leading to severe emotional distress, anxiety, depression, and even suicidal ideation. The anonymity afforded by the internet emboldens perpetrators, who might otherwise be deterred by the potential consequences of their actions in face-to-face interactions. This anonymity makes it difficult to hold cyberbullies accountable and provides them with a sense of impunity.

One of the most insidious aspects of cyberbullying is its relentless nature. Unlike traditional bullying, which might be confined to school or specific social settings, cyberbullying can intrude into every part of a victim's life. Victims can be targeted at any time and place, leaving them with no safe haven. The psychological impact of knowing that harassment can occur at any moment can lead to chronic stress and fear, severely impacting the victim's mental health and overall quality of life.

The widespread use of social media platforms has exacerbated the prevalence and impact of cyberbullying. These platforms are designed to maximize user engagement, often at the expense of user well-being.

Features such as likes, shares, and comments can be weaponized to amplify harassment and humiliation. For instance, derogatory posts can go viral, subjecting victims to mass ridicule and social ostracization. The permanence of online content means that harmful material can resurface repeatedly, prolonging the victim's suffering.

Cyberbullying also poses significant risks to physical health. The stress and anxiety resulting from persistent harassment can lead to various physical symptoms, including headaches, sleep disturbances, and gastrointestinal issues. Furthermore, the psychological toll of cyberbullying can contribute to unhealthy coping mechanisms such as substance abuse and self-harm. The compounded effects of these physical and mental health issues can severely impair a victim's ability to function in daily life, affecting their academic performance, social relationships, and future opportunities.

Addressing the issue of cyberbullying requires a multifaceted approach involving individuals, families, schools, communities, social media platforms, and policymakers. Education and awareness are critical components of prevention. Teaching young people about the responsible use of technology, digital citizenship, and the impact of their online behavior can help reduce the incidence of cyberbullying. Schools can incorporate comprehensive anti-bullying programs that include cyberbullying, emphasizing empathy, respect, and the importance of standing up against harassment.

Parents and guardians play a vital role in protecting children from cyberbullying. Open communication about online activities and experiences is essential. Parents should encourage their children to share any negative online interactions and provide support and guidance on how to handle such situations. Monitoring online behavior and setting clear rules for internet use can also help prevent exposure to harmful content and interactions. Additionally, parents can educate themselves about the digital landscape, staying informed about the latest apps, games, and social media platforms their children use.

Social media platforms and technology companies have a responsibility to create safer online environments. Implementing robust reporting and blocking mechanisms is crucial for allowing users to protect themselves from harassment. Platforms should also enforce strict community guidelines against bullying and harassment, with clear consequences for violators. Advanced algorithms and artificial intelligence can be employed to detect and flag harmful content proactively. Moreover, platforms can provide resources and support for victims of cyberbullying, including access to counseling and mental health services.

Legal measures can also play a significant role in combating cyberbullying. Many jurisdictions have enacted laws specifically targeting online harassment and cyberbullying, providing legal recourse for victims and penalties for perpetrators. These laws can act as a deterrent, holding cyberbullies accountable for their actions. However, the effectiveness of legal measures depends on their enforcement and the ability of law enforcement agencies to navigate the complexities of the digital landscape. International cooperation is often necessary to address cases that cross national boundaries, given the global nature of the internet.

Community involvement is essential in creating a culture that condemns cyberbullying and supports victims. Public awareness campaigns can highlight the seriousness of the issue and promote positive online behavior. Community organizations and local governments can collaborate to provide resources, workshops, and support networks for those affected by cyberbullying. Peer support programs can be particularly effective, as they empower young people to support each other and take a stand against bullying in their social circles.

Victims of cyberbullying need access to comprehensive support services to help them cope with the emotional and psychological impact of their experiences. Counseling and mental health services can provide a safe space for victims to process their feelings and develop coping strategies. Support groups can offer a sense of community and understanding, reducing feelings of isolation. Schools and workplaces can provide resources and accommodations to help victims manage the effects of cyberbullying on their daily lives.

Chapter 12: The Art of Trolling

The phenomenon of trolling on the internet is a complex and multifaceted behavior that has garnered significant attention in the digital age. Trolling, broadly defined, involves posting inflammatory, off-topic, or provocative messages online with the intent to provoke, disrupt, or elicit strong emotional reactions from others. This behavior can occur across various platforms, including social media, forums, comment sections, and gaming communities. Understanding the troll mindset requires a deep dive into the psychological, social, and cultural factors that drive individuals to engage in such disruptive activities.

At its core, trolling is often rooted in a desire for attention and recognition. Trolls derive satisfaction from the reactions they elicit, whether it be anger, frustration, or amusement. This behavior is closely linked to the concept of "attention-seeking," where the primary goal is to become the center of focus in a given online environment. For many trolls, the validation comes not from positive feedback but from the chaos and disruption they cause. The more significant the reaction, the greater the sense of accomplishment.

The anonymity provided by the internet plays a crucial role in enabling trolling behavior. When individuals operate behind pseudonyms or anonymous accounts, they feel a sense of detachment from their real-world identity. This anonymity reduces the perceived consequences of their actions, emboldening them to engage in behavior they might avoid in face-to-face interactions. The lack of accountability allows trolls to push boundaries and explore their darker impulses without fear of repercussions.

Psychologically, trolling can be understood through various theories and frameworks. One such framework is the concept of the "dark tetrad" of personality traits, which includes narcissism, Machiavellianism, psychopathy, and sadism. Studies have shown that individuals who score high on these traits are more likely to engage in trolling. Narcissism, characterized by an inflated sense of self-importance and a need for admiration, drives trolls to seek attention and validation. Machiavellianism, which involves manipulation and deceit, enables trolls to craft elaborate schemes and tactics to provoke reactions. Psychopathy, marked by a lack of empathy and remorse, allows trolls to disregard the emotional impact of their actions on others. Sadism, the enjoyment of inflicting pain or discomfort on others, provides a direct source of pleasure for trolls as they witness the distress they cause.

Social dynamics also play a significant role in trolling behavior. Online environments often lack the social norms and regulatory mechanisms present in real-world interactions. This absence of norms creates a space where deviant behavior can flourish. Additionally, the group dynamics of online communities can contribute to trolling. When trolls operate within a community of like-minded individuals, their behavior is reinforced and validated. Groupthink and mob mentality can lead to an escalation of trolling activities, as individuals feel supported and encouraged by their peers.

The culture of certain online spaces can further perpetuate trolling behavior. Some forums and communities have developed a reputation for being hostile and combative, where trolling is not only tolerated but celebrated. In these environments, trolling becomes a form of performance art, where wit, humor, and creativity are used to outdo others in a contest of provocation. This cultural acceptance of trolling can attract individuals who enjoy the challenge and thrill of engaging in such behavior.

The motivations behind trolling can vary widely among individuals. For some, it is a form of entertainment and a way to pass the time. The thrill of engaging in a battle of wits and outsmarting others can be a source of enjoyment. For others, trolling is a means of expressing frustration or dissatisfaction with certain topics, communities, or individuals. Political and social issues often become targets for trolls, who seek to disrupt conversations and sow discord. In some cases, trolling is driven by a desire for revenge or retaliation against perceived slights or injustices.

Trolling can have significant negative impacts on both individuals and online communities. For individuals, being the target of trolling can lead to emotional distress, anxiety, and a sense of violation. The relentless nature of online harassment can have serious mental health consequences, including depression and suicidal ideation. For online communities, trolling can disrupt constructive discussions, create a hostile environment, and drive away valuable members. The overall quality of discourse suffers as attention shifts from meaningful interactions to managing and responding to trolls.

Efforts to combat trolling involve a combination of technical, social, and psychological strategies. On a technical level, platforms can implement tools and algorithms to detect and mitigate trolling behavior. Features such as comment moderation, reporting mechanisms, and automated filters can help reduce the visibility and impact of trolling. However, these measures are not foolproof and can sometimes lead to false positives, where legitimate content is mistakenly flagged as trolling.

Social strategies involve fostering a positive and inclusive online culture where trolling is not tolerated. Community guidelines and norms play a crucial role in setting expectations for behavior. Clear and consistent enforcement of these guidelines can deter potential trolls and create a safer environment for users. Encouraging positive interactions and highlighting constructive contributions can shift the focus away from trolls and toward meaningful engagement.

Psychological strategies involve understanding and addressing the underlying motivations of trolls. Educating users about the impact of trolling and promoting empathy and digital citizenship can help reduce the prevalence of such behavior. Providing support and resources for individuals targeted by trolls can mitigate the negative effects and empower them to handle online harassment.

47

Chapter 13: Privacy Matters: Guarding Your Digital Footprint

In the digital age, privacy has become an increasingly critical concern as our lives become more intertwined with technology. Every action we take online, from browsing websites and shopping to social media interactions and sending emails, contributes to our digital footprint. This digital footprint is a trail of data that can be collected, analyzed, and potentially exploited by various entities, including corporations, governments, and malicious actors. Understanding the importance of privacy and the strategies for guarding your digital footprint is essential for maintaining control over your personal information and protecting your overall well-being.

Privacy matters for several reasons. First and foremost, it is a fundamental human right. The right to privacy is enshrined in numerous international agreements and national constitutions, recognizing the need for individuals to have control over their personal information. Privacy enables people to express themselves freely, make autonomous decisions, and engage in activities without fear of surveillance or judgment. In a digital context, maintaining privacy ensures that individuals can interact online without being constantly monitored or having their data misused.

One of the primary concerns regarding digital privacy is the sheer volume of data generated by our online activities. Every click, search query, and interaction can be tracked and recorded. This data can reveal a great deal about an individual's preferences, habits, beliefs, and behaviors. Companies often collect this information to create detailed profiles for targeted advertising, while governments may use it for surveillance and law enforcement purposes. Additionally, cybercriminals seek to exploit personal data for identity theft, financial fraud, and other malicious activities.

The collection and analysis of personal data by corporations, often referred to as data mining or data harvesting, has become a lucrative industry. Companies like Google, Facebook, and Amazon gather vast amounts of information about their users to tailor advertisements and services. While this can enhance user experience by providing personalized content, it also raises significant privacy concerns. Users often unknowingly consent to extensive data collection through complex and opaque privacy policies. This lack of transparency makes it challenging for individuals to understand what data is being collected, how it is used, and who it is shared with.

Social media platforms are particularly notorious for data collection. Users voluntarily share a wealth of personal information, from photos and status updates to location data and personal interests. This information is not only accessible to the platform operators but also to third-party advertisers and, in some cases, other users. The potential for misuse is high, as seen in numerous scandals involving data breaches and unauthorized data sharing. For instance, the Cambridge Analytica scandal revealed how data from millions of Facebook users was harvested without consent and used for political advertising.

Beyond commercial exploitation, governments around the world have increasingly engaged in digital surveillance. In the name of national security and law enforcement, agencies monitor online communications, track individuals' online activities, and collect vast amounts of data. While some level of surveillance may be necessary for security purposes, the lack of oversight and transparency often leads to abuses of power. Revelations by whistleblowers like Edward Snowden have highlighted the extent of government surveillance and its implications for individual privacy and civil liberties.

The risks associated with a compromised digital footprint extend to identity theft and financial fraud. Personal information, such as social security numbers, credit card details, and login credentials, can be stolen through data breaches or phishing attacks. Once this information is in the hands of cybercriminals, it can be used to make unauthorized transactions, open fraudulent accounts, and commit other forms of identity theft. The consequences for victims can be severe, including financial loss, damage to credit scores, and the lengthy process of restoring their identity.

Given these risks, it is crucial to take proactive measures to guard your digital footprint. One of the most effective strategies is to manage privacy settings on online accounts and devices. Many websites and apps offer privacy controls that allow users to limit the amount of data collected and shared. For example, social media platforms typically provide options to control who can see your posts, who can contact you, and what information is visible on your profile. Regularly reviewing and updating these settings can help protect your personal information.

Using strong, unique passwords for different accounts is another essential practice. Password managers can generate and store complex passwords, reducing the risk of unauthorized access. Enabling two-factor authentication (2FA) adds an extra layer of security by requiring a second form of verification, such as a code sent to your phone, in addition to your password. This makes it more difficult for attackers to gain access to your accounts, even if they have your password.

Be cautious about the information you share online. Limit the amount of personal information you post on social media and other public platforms. Be mindful of sharing sensitive details, such as your home address, phone number, and financial information. When using websites and apps, consider whether the requested information is necessary and how it will be used. If in doubt, avoid sharing or provide minimal information.

Regularly monitoring your online presence is also important. Conduct periodic searches of your name and other personal information to see what information is publicly available. Set up alerts for your name or other key terms to be notified of new mentions. This can help you identify and address potential privacy issues early on. Additionally, review your digital footprint by checking which apps and services have access to your data and revoke permissions for those you no longer use or trust.

Using privacy-focused tools and services can enhance your digital security. Virtual private networks (VPNs) can mask your IP address and encrypt your internet connection, making it more difficult for third parties to track your online activities. Privacy-focused browsers, such as Mozilla Firefox or Brave, offer enhanced privacy features, including ad blockers and tracking protection. Search engines like DuckDuckGo do not track user queries, providing a more private search experience.

Educating yourself about common online threats and best practices for digital security is crucial. Phishing attacks, for example, often involve fraudulent emails or messages designed to trick individuals into revealing personal information or clicking on malicious links. Being able to recognize these attacks and knowing how to respond can prevent data breaches and other security incidents. Staying informed about the latest privacy and security developments can help you adapt to new threats and protect your digital footprint effectively.

Advocating for stronger privacy protections and regulations is another important aspect of safeguarding your digital footprint. Support initiatives and organizations that promote digital privacy and security. Engage with policymakers and participate in public discussions about privacy issues. Stronger legal frameworks can provide greater transparency, accountability, and protection for individuals' personal information.

Chapter 14: The Rise of Fake News: Trusting What You See

The rise of fake news represents one of the most pressing challenges in the modern information landscape, fundamentally altering the way we consume, interpret, and trust information. This phenomenon has far-reaching implications for society, politics, and personal relationships, necessitating a comprehensive understanding of its origins, mechanisms, impacts, and strategies for mitigation.

Fake news refers to false or misleading information presented as legitimate news. It can take many forms, including fabricated stories, manipulated images, and deceptive videos, and is disseminated with the intent to mislead, deceive, or manipulate public opinion. The rise of fake news can be attributed to several key factors, including the proliferation of digital media, the decline of traditional journalism, the role of social media platforms, and the psychological tendencies of individuals.

The digital revolution has drastically transformed the media landscape, enabling the rapid and widespread dissemination of information. The internet and digital technologies have lowered the barriers to entry for content creation, allowing anyone with an internet connection to publish and share information. While this democratization of information has many positive aspects, it has also facilitated the spread of fake news. Unlike traditional media, which often undergoes rigorous editorial processes, digital content can be produced and distributed with little to no oversight. This has created an environment where false information can easily circulate and gain traction.

The decline of traditional journalism has further exacerbated the problem. Financial pressures and changing consumption habits have led to the downsizing of newsrooms and the closure of many local newspapers. As a result, there are fewer professional journalists to investigate and verify information. The competition for audience attention has driven many news organizations to prioritize speed and sensationalism over accuracy and depth, sometimes leading to the unintentional spread of misinformation. This erosion of journalistic standards has created a vacuum that fake news purveyors have been quick to fill.

Social media platforms play a critical role in the rise and spread of fake news. Platforms like Facebook, Twitter, and YouTube are designed to maximize user engagement by prioritizing content that generates high levels of interaction. Unfortunately, sensationalist and emotionally charged content, which often includes fake news, tends to attract more attention and engagement than factual reporting. The algorithms that govern these platforms amplify such content, creating echo chambers where users are exposed to information that reinforces their existing beliefs. This phenomenon, known as confirmation bias, makes individuals more susceptible to fake news.

Psychological factors also contribute to the spread and acceptance of fake news. Humans are wired to seek out information that aligns with their preexisting beliefs and to dismiss information that contradicts them. This cognitive bias, coupled with the sheer volume of information available online, makes it difficult for individuals to critically evaluate the veracity of the content they encounter. The Dunning-Kruger effect, where individuals with limited knowledge overestimate their understanding, can lead people to believe and share fake news without recognizing their own informational shortcomings.

The impact of fake news on society is profound and multifaceted. One of the most significant consequences is the erosion of trust in media and institutions. As fake news spreads, it becomes increasingly difficult for individuals to distinguish between credible and non-credible sources. This leads to a general skepticism toward all information, undermining public trust in journalism, government, and other institutions. The decline in trust can have serious implications for democratic processes, as informed citizenry is essential for the functioning of democracy.

Fake news also has tangible effects on public opinion and behavior. During elections, for example, false information can sway voters and influence the outcome. In the 2016 U.S. presidential election, the dissemination of fake news stories played a notable role in shaping public perceptions and voting behavior. Similarly, during the COVID-19 pandemic, misinformation about the virus and vaccines contributed to widespread confusion and reluctance to follow public health guidelines, hindering efforts to control the spread of the virus.

The social fabric is also strained by the proliferation of fake news. False information can deepen societal divisions by polarizing public opinion and exacerbating conflicts. For example, fake news related to sensitive issues such as race, immigration, and religion can inflame tensions and incite violence. The deliberate spread of false information by malicious actors, including foreign governments, aims to destabilize societies by sowing discord and distrust.

Addressing the problem of fake news requires a multifaceted approach involving technological solutions, media literacy, regulatory measures, and individual responsibility. Technological solutions include the development of algorithms and tools to detect and flag fake news. Social media platforms have begun to implement measures such as fact-checking partnerships, user reporting mechanisms, and content moderation to curb the spread of misinformation. However, these efforts face significant challenges, including the sheer scale of content, the difficulty of distinguishing satire or opinion from falsehoods, and concerns about censorship and free speech.

Media literacy is another crucial component in combating fake news. Educating the public about how to critically evaluate information, identify credible sources, and recognize misinformation can empower individuals to make informed decisions. Media literacy programs can be integrated into school curricula and public awareness campaigns to reach a broad audience. Teaching individuals to question the sources of information, cross-check facts, and be aware of their own biases can help build resilience against fake news.

Regulatory measures can also play a role in addressing fake news, although they must be carefully balanced to protect freedom of expression. Governments can implement policies that promote transparency and accountability in digital media. For example, regulations requiring platforms to disclose their algorithms and the criteria used for content moderation can help ensure that these processes are fair and transparent. Additionally, laws against the deliberate spread of false information, particularly when it poses a threat to public safety or national security, can deter malicious actors.

Individual responsibility is equally important in the fight against fake news. As consumers of information, individuals must take an active role in verifying the content they encounter and sharing only credible information. Simple actions, such as checking the source of a news story, looking for corroborating evidence, and being skeptical of sensationalist claims, can significantly reduce the spread of fake news. Social media users should be mindful of the impact their shares and likes have on the visibility of content and strive to promote accurate and reliable information.

Chapter 15: Social Media Activism

Social media activism has emerged as a powerful tool for advocacy and mobilization in the digital age. Platforms like Twitter, Facebook, and Instagram provide individuals and organizations with the ability to reach vast audiences, raise awareness about important issues, and galvanize support for various causes. However, this form of activism is not without its critics. The debate over whether social media activism leads to real change or is merely a form of virtue signaling is complex and multifaceted. To fully understand this phenomenon, it is essential to examine its mechanisms, impacts, and the factors that differentiate genuine activism from performative acts.

Social media activism refers to the use of online platforms to promote social, political, and environmental causes. It encompasses a wide range of activities, including sharing information, organizing events, fundraising, and lobbying for policy changes. One of the key strengths of social media activism is its ability to quickly disseminate information and mobilize people. Hashtags like #BlackLivesMatter, #MeToo, and #ClimateStrike have played pivotal roles in drawing global attention to issues of racial injustice, sexual harassment, and climate change. These movements demonstrate the potential of social media to amplify marginalized voices and create a sense of solidarity among supporters.

The speed and reach of social media make it an effective tool for raising awareness. In traditional activism, spreading information and rallying support often requires significant time and resources. Social media, by contrast, allows activists to bypass traditional gatekeepers, such as media outlets and political institutions, and directly engage with a broad audience. This democratization of information can lead to rapid shifts in public opinion and increase pressure on decision-makers to address the highlighted issues. For example, the viral spread of videos documenting police brutality has heightened public scrutiny and spurred calls for police reform in many countries.

Social media also facilitates the organization and coordination of protests, boycotts, and other forms of collective action. Platforms like Facebook and Twitter can be used to plan events, share logistical information, and keep participants informed in real-time. This capability was evident during the Arab Spring, where social media played a crucial role in organizing protests and disseminating information amidst government censorship. Similarly, the Women's March in 2017, which drew millions of participants worldwide, was largely coordinated through social media.

Fundraising is another area where social media activism has proven effective. Crowdfunding platforms and social media campaigns enable activists to raise funds for their causes from a global audience. This financial support can be crucial for grassroots organizations and movements that lack traditional funding sources. Campaigns like #GivingTuesday leverage social media to encourage donations and have successfully raised millions of dollars for various charitable causes.

Despite these strengths, social media activism faces significant criticism, particularly regarding its effectiveness in achieving substantive change. One of the primary criticisms is that it often amounts to virtue signaling rather than genuine activism. Virtue signaling refers to the act of publicly expressing opinions or sentiments to demonstrate one's good character or moral correctness, rather than to take meaningful action. In the context of social media, this can involve sharing posts, using hashtags, or changing profile pictures to show support for a cause without engaging in deeper, sustained efforts to address the issue.

Critics argue that virtue signaling can create an illusion of engagement and progress, while diverting attention and resources away from more impactful actions. For instance, sharing a hashtag or signing an online petition may provide a sense of participation and moral satisfaction but does little to effect real-world change. This performative aspect of social media activism can dilute the efforts of genuine activists and lead to slacktivism—minimal effort activities that give the impression of activism without requiring significant time, effort, or risk.

Another concern is that social media activism can foster a reactive, rather than proactive, approach to social issues. The fast-paced nature of social media often prioritizes immediate, sensational content over thoughtful, long-term strategies for change. This can result in a focus on short-term gains and viral moments, rather than sustained advocacy and systemic change. Movements that rely heavily on social media may struggle to maintain momentum once the initial wave of online enthusiasm subsides. The challenge of sustaining engagement is compounded by the transient nature of social media trends, where public attention quickly shifts from one issue to another.

The echo chamber effect is another limitation of social media activism. Social media algorithms tend to promote content that aligns with users' existing beliefs and preferences, creating echo chambers where individuals are exposed primarily to information that reinforces their views. This can limit the reach of activist messages to like-minded individuals and hinder efforts to build broad-based coalitions necessary for substantial change. Additionally, the polarized nature of online discourse can lead to divisive and antagonistic interactions, reducing opportunities for constructive dialogue and consensus-building.

Moreover, social media activism is often met with significant resistance and backlash. Online platforms provide a space for counter-movements and trolls who seek to undermine and discredit activist efforts. Harassment, doxxing, and coordinated disinformation campaigns can target activists, discouraging participation and silencing voices. The anonymity and reach of the internet make it a fertile ground for such hostile activities, which can have real-world consequences for those involved.

Despite these challenges, there are instances where social media activism has contributed to meaningful change. The #MeToo movement, for example, not only raised awareness about sexual harassment and assault but also led to tangible consequences for perpetrators and changes in workplace policies and legislation. Similarly, the global climate strikes inspired by Greta Thunberg's activism have brought climate change to the forefront of political agendas and influenced policy discussions. These examples illustrate that when social media activism is combined with offline actions and sustained efforts, it can be a powerful force for change.

To maximize the effectiveness of social media activism, several strategies can be employed. First, activists should aim to complement online activities with offline efforts. This can include organizing physical events, engaging in community outreach, and collaborating with established organizations that have the capacity for long-term advocacy. By bridging the gap between online and offline activism, movements can build stronger, more resilient networks and sustain momentum over time.

Second, it is important to prioritize education and awareness-building. Social media platforms can be used to share in-depth information, resources, and tools that empower individuals to take informed action. Providing context, historical background, and actionable steps can help transform passive supporters into active participants. Educational campaigns can also counteract misinformation and provide clarity on complex issues.

Third, fostering inclusivity and intersectionality within activist movements is crucial. Social media activism should strive to amplify diverse voices and ensure that marginalized communities are represented and heard. This involves actively listening to and engaging with those most affected by the issues at hand. Inclusive movements are more likely to build broad-based support and address systemic inequalities effectively.

Fourth, activists should be mindful of the ethical implications of their actions. This includes being transparent about funding sources, avoiding exploitative or performative tactics, and respecting the privacy and dignity of individuals involved. Ethical activism builds trust and credibility, which are essential for sustaining support and achieving long-term goals.

Finally, there is a need for greater accountability and regulation of social media platforms. Tech companies have a responsibility to address the spread of misinformation, hate speech, and harassment on their platforms. Implementing robust content moderation policies, providing support for targeted individuals, and ensuring algorithmic transparency can help create a safer and more conducive environment for genuine activism.

Chapter 16: The Business of Social Media

The business of social media has revolutionized marketing, transforming how companies reach and engage with consumers. This new paradigm leverages the power of digital platforms to create personalized, interactive, and data-driven marketing strategies. Understanding the intricate landscape of social media marketing is crucial for businesses aiming to thrive in the digital age.

At the core of social media marketing lies the understanding of various platforms and their unique characteristics. Each social media platform—Facebook, Instagram, Twitter, LinkedIn, TikTok, Snapchat, and others—offers distinct features and caters to different demographics and user behaviors. Effective marketing strategies are tailored to these specific environments. Facebook, for example, excels in reaching a broad audience with diverse interests through its sophisticated advertising tools. Instagram, with its visual-centric nature, is ideal for brands focusing on lifestyle and aesthetics. LinkedIn caters to a professional audience, making it suitable for B2B marketing and thought leadership. TikTok, with its short-form video content, appeals to a younger demographic and fosters viral trends.

Successful social media marketing begins with a comprehensive strategy that aligns with a brand's goals and objectives. This strategy encompasses several key elements: identifying the target audience, setting clear goals, creating compelling content, engaging with the audience, and analyzing performance metrics.

Identifying the target audience is foundational. Brands must understand who their potential customers are, what they value, their behaviors, and their preferred platforms. This involves demographic analysis, psychographic profiling, and understanding user personas. Tools like Facebook Audience Insights and Google Analytics provide valuable data to pinpoint target demographics.

Setting clear goals is the next step. Goals should be specific, measurable, achievable, relevant, and time-bound (SMART). Common social media marketing goals include increasing brand awareness, driving website traffic, generating leads, boosting sales, and enhancing customer loyalty. Each goal dictates different strategies and metrics for success.

Content creation is at the heart of social media marketing. Compelling content attracts and retains the audience's attention, fosters engagement, and drives action. Content can take various forms—images, videos, blogs, infographics, podcasts, and user-generated content. The key is to create content that resonates with the audience, provides value, and aligns with the brand's voice and messaging.

Visual content is particularly powerful on social media. High-quality images and videos capture attention more effectively than text alone. Video content, in particular, has seen explosive growth, with platforms like YouTube, Instagram Stories, and TikTok driving this trend. Live streaming has also gained popularity, allowing brands to connect with audiences in real-time, showcase events, and provide behind-the-scenes glimpses.

User-generated content (UGC) is another valuable asset. Encouraging customers to share their experiences with a brand fosters community, builds trust, and provides authentic content. UGC can be incentivized through contests, hashtags, and featuring customer posts on the brand's channels.

Engagement is crucial for building relationships and fostering loyalty. Social media is not a one-way communication channel; it requires interaction and responsiveness. Brands should actively engage with their audience by responding to comments, answering questions, and participating in conversations. This builds a sense of community and demonstrates that the brand values its customers.

Influencer marketing has become a significant component of social media strategies. Influencers, with their large and engaged followings, can amplify a brand's message and reach new audiences. Collaborating with influencers involves identifying individuals who align with the brand's values, negotiating partnerships, and co-creating content that resonates with both the influencer's and the brand's audiences. Micro-influencers, with smaller but highly engaged followings, can also be effective, offering more authentic and niche engagement.

Paid advertising is a powerful tool for amplifying reach and targeting specific audiences. Social media platforms offer sophisticated advertising options, including demographic targeting, retargeting, and lookalike audiences. These tools enable brands to deliver personalized ads to users based on their behaviors, interests, and interactions. Facebook Ads Manager, for example, allows for detailed targeting, budget optimization, and performance tracking.

Analytics and performance measurement are integral to refining social media strategies. Brands must track key performance indicators (KPIs) such as engagement rates, click-through rates, conversion rates, and return on investment (ROI). Tools like Google Analytics, Hootsuite, and platform-specific insights (e.g., Facebook Insights, Twitter Analytics) provide data to assess the effectiveness of campaigns and guide adjustments.

A critical aspect of social media marketing is staying attuned to trends and evolving user behaviors. Social media is dynamic, with trends shifting rapidly. Brands need to be agile, ready to adapt their strategies to leverage new features, platforms, and consumer preferences. For instance, the rise of ephemeral content (e.g., Instagram Stories, Snapchat) has prompted brands to create more timely and engaging content that fosters a sense of urgency.

Storytelling is a powerful technique in social media marketing. Brands that tell compelling stories connect with audiences on an emotional level, making their messages more memorable and impactful. Storytelling can humanize a brand, showcase its values, and create a narrative that resonates with consumers. Nike's "Just Do It" campaign is a prime example of using storytelling to inspire and engage audiences.

Community building is another vital aspect. Successful brands cultivate communities where users feel connected and engaged. This involves creating spaces for dialogue, encouraging user participation, and fostering a sense of belonging. Communities can be built around shared interests, values, or causes, providing a platform for meaningful interactions.

The rise of social commerce has added a new dimension to social media marketing. Platforms like Instagram and Facebook have integrated shopping features, allowing users to purchase products directly from posts and stories. This seamless shopping experience combines content discovery with instant purchasing, driving sales and enhancing the customer journey.

Transparency and authenticity are increasingly important in social media marketing. Consumers today value honesty and expect brands to be transparent about their practices, values, and intentions. Brands that are open about their processes, admit mistakes, and engage in genuine dialogue build trust and loyalty. Authenticity involves being true to the brand's identity and values, avoiding overly polished or insincere messaging.

Navigating crises and managing reputation are crucial components of social media strategies. In the age of instant communication, brands must be prepared to respond quickly and effectively to crises. This involves having a crisis management plan, monitoring social media channels for potential issues, and engaging transparently and empathetically with affected audiences.

Ethical considerations are also paramount in social media marketing. Brands must navigate issues such as data privacy, misinformation, and ethical advertising practices. Respecting user privacy, avoiding manipulative tactics, and promoting accurate information are essential for maintaining integrity and trust.

The global nature of social media presents both opportunities and challenges. Brands can reach international audiences, but they must also navigate cultural differences and varying regulations. Localization—adapting content to different languages, cultures, and contexts—is critical for resonating with diverse audiences.

Innovation and experimentation are key to staying ahead in social media marketing. Brands should be willing to test new ideas, explore emerging platforms, and leverage cutting-edge technologies. Augmented reality (AR), virtual reality (VR), and artificial intelligence (AI) are examples of technologies that can enhance social media experiences and create unique engagement opportunities.

Chapter 17: Meme Culture: The Language of the Internet

Meme culture, often referred to as the language of the internet, is a unique and pervasive phenomenon that has reshaped how people communicate online. At its core, a meme is a piece of media—typically an image, video, or text—that is spread rapidly by internet users, often with variations and new interpretations. The concept of a meme predates the internet, originally coined by Richard Dawkins in his 1976 book "The Selfish Gene" to describe how ideas and cultural phenomena spread. However, in the digital age, memes have evolved into a dynamic and influential form of online expression.

Memes function as a form of shorthand communication, conveying complex ideas, emotions, and cultural references in a highly accessible and often humorous way. They are participatory by nature, inviting users to share, adapt, and remix content to suit their own purposes. This adaptability is a key aspect of their appeal and power. Memes can serve as a commentary on current events, social issues, or everyday experiences, making them a versatile tool for expression.

One of the defining characteristics of meme culture is its rapid pace. The internet allows memes to spread with incredible speed, often going viral in a matter of hours. Platforms like Twitter, Reddit, Instagram, and TikTok are hotspots for meme creation and dissemination. A single meme can reach millions of people across the globe, transcending language and cultural barriers. This speed and reach make memes a potent force in shaping public opinion and discourse.

Memes often rely on a shared understanding of certain cultural touchstones. They can reference popular movies, TV shows, music, or even other memes. This creates a sense of community among those who "get" the reference, fostering a feeling of belonging and shared identity.

However, this can also be exclusionary, as those who are not in on the joke may feel left out or confused.

The humor in memes often hinges on irony, sarcasm, and absurdity. This can be both a strength and a weakness. On one hand, it allows for a wide range of creative expression and the ability to tackle serious subjects with a light touch. On the other hand, it can lead to misunderstandings and misinterpretations, especially when memes are taken out of context. The irony and detachment that characterize many memes can sometimes blur the line between genuine sentiment and mockery.

Memes also play a significant role in political and social discourse. They can be powerful tools for activism, raising awareness about issues and rallying support for causes. The 2011 Arab Spring, for instance, saw the use of memes to disseminate information and galvanize protestors. In more recent years, movements like Black Lives Matter have utilized memes to spread their messages and mobilize supporters. However, the same tools can be used for negative purposes. Memes can be employed to spread misinformation, hate speech, and extremist propaganda. The anonymity and rapid spread of the internet can amplify harmful content, making it difficult to control.

The commercial aspect of meme culture is also significant. Brands and marketers have recognized the power of memes to engage with audiences and drive viral marketing campaigns. Successful meme-based marketing can generate immense publicity and brand loyalty. However, there is a fine line between clever engagement and appearing out of touch or exploitative. When brands attempt to co-opt meme culture without understanding its nuances, they risk alienating their audience and becoming the subject of ridicule.

Another important aspect of meme culture is its impact on mental health and well-being. While memes can provide a source of humor and community, they can also contribute to a culture of comparison and unrealistic expectations. The curated nature of social media, where memes often present an idealized or exaggerated version of reality, can lead to feelings of inadequacy and anxiety. Additionally, the rapid consumption of meme content can contribute to a culture of instant gratification and short attention spans.

The legal and ethical implications of meme culture are complex and evolving. Issues of copyright and intellectual property frequently arise, as memes often involve the use of images, videos, and text that belong to others. While the transformative nature of memes can sometimes provide a defense under fair use laws, this is not always clear-cut. The ethical considerations are equally challenging, as memes can perpetuate stereotypes, reinforce harmful narratives, and contribute to online harassment and bullying.

The influence of meme culture on language and communication is profound. Memes have introduced new vocabulary and expressions into everyday speech, with phrases like "lol," "brb," and "tbh" originating from internet slang and now commonly used in offline conversations. They have also influenced the way people write and present information, with a preference for brevity, wit, and visual elements.

In education and academia, memes have been recognized as both a teaching tool and a subject of study. Educators use memes to engage students and make learning more relatable, while scholars analyze meme culture to understand its impact on society, communication, and politics. The study of memes intersects with fields such as cultural studies, linguistics, media studies, and sociology, offering rich insights into contemporary digital culture.

As meme culture continues to evolve, it reflects broader trends in society and technology. The rise of artificial intelligence and machine learning has introduced new possibilities for meme creation, with algorithms generating content that mimics human creativity. Virtual and augmented reality technologies may also shape the future of memes, creating new forms of interactive and immersive experiences.

Chapter 18: Personal Branding: Crafting Your Online Persona

Personal branding, the process of crafting and managing your online persona, has become increasingly significant in the digital age. With the rise of social media, professional networking sites, and personal blogs, individuals have more platforms than ever to showcase their skills, experiences, and unique qualities to a global audience. Personal branding involves strategically presenting yourself to create a specific image or identity in the minds of others, whether for career advancement, business growth, or personal fulfillment.

At its core, personal branding is about authenticity. It's not just about projecting a polished image but about genuinely representing who you are, what you stand for, and what makes you unique. This authenticity builds trust and credibility, which are essential for any successful personal brand. To craft an effective personal brand, one must first engage in self-reflection to understand their strengths, values, passions, and goals. This self-awareness forms the foundation of a brand that is both authentic and compelling.

A key component of personal branding is defining your unique value proposition (UVP). Your UVP is what sets you apart from others in your field; it's the unique combination of skills, experiences, and perspectives that you bring to the table. Clearly articulating your UVP helps others understand why they should engage with you, whether as an employer, client, collaborator, or follower. Crafting a strong UVP requires a deep understanding of your target audience and what they value, as well as an honest assessment of your own capabilities and achievements.

Once you have a clear sense of your UVP, the next step is to communicate it effectively across various online platforms. Social media profiles, personal websites, and professional networking sites like LinkedIn are essential tools for building and maintaining your personal brand. Each platform has its own strengths and audiences, so it's important to tailor your content and engagement strategies accordingly. Consistency across these platforms is crucial; your brand should be recognizable and coherent, whether someone is viewing your LinkedIn profile, reading your blog, or following you on Twitter.

Content creation is a powerful way to showcase your expertise and engage with your audience. This can take many forms, including blog posts, articles, videos, podcasts, and social media updates. High-quality, valuable content not only demonstrates your knowledge and skills but also provides opportunities for others to engage with you and share your work, amplifying your reach and influence. Regularly creating and sharing content helps keep your audience engaged and positions you as a thought leader in your field.

Networking is another critical aspect of personal branding. Building relationships with others in your industry, as well as with potential clients or employers, can open doors to new opportunities and collaborations. Online networking can be facilitated through social media interactions, participation in online communities and forums, and engagement with others' content. In addition to online networking, offline networking events, conferences, and meetups are also valuable for building and strengthening relationships.

Managing your online reputation is a continuous process that requires vigilance and proactive efforts. This includes monitoring what is being said about you online, responding to feedback, and addressing any negative content or misinformation that may arise. Tools such as Google Alerts and social media monitoring platforms can help you stay informed about your online presence. Being responsive and professional in your interactions can mitigate potential damage and demonstrate your commitment to maintaining a positive and trustworthy brand.

Visual identity is an often overlooked but important component of personal branding. This includes elements such as your profile picture, website design, and any other visual content you produce. A cohesive and professional visual identity helps reinforce your brand and make it more memorable. Investing in high-quality visuals and ensuring consistency in style and presentation can significantly enhance the perception of your brand.

Personal branding is not just for entrepreneurs or public figures; it is increasingly important for professionals across all industries. In today's competitive job market, a strong personal brand can differentiate you from other candidates and make you more attractive to potential employers. It can also provide leverage for negotiating promotions, raises, and other career advancements. For freelancers and business owners, a strong personal brand can attract clients and build a loyal customer base.

However, personal branding also comes with challenges and potential pitfalls. One of the primary challenges is balancing authenticity with strategic presentation. It can be tempting to curate an idealized version of yourself that may not fully reflect reality. While this might yield short-term gains, it can ultimately undermine trust and credibility if discrepancies between your online persona and real-life actions are revealed. Striking the right balance between authenticity and professionalism is key to building a sustainable personal brand.

Another challenge is managing the boundaries between personal and professional life. As personal branding often involves sharing aspects of your personal life, it is important to establish clear boundaries to protect your privacy and well-being. Deciding what to share and what to keep private requires careful consideration and a clear understanding of your brand's goals and values.

The dynamic nature of the internet means that personal branding is an ongoing process. Trends and platforms evolve, audience preferences shift, and new opportunities and challenges arise. Staying relevant requires continuous learning, adaptation, and a willingness to experiment with new strategies and technologies. This adaptability is crucial for maintaining a strong and effective personal brand over the long term.

The rise of influencer culture has further highlighted the power and potential of personal branding. Influencers, who have built substantial followings by sharing their lives, opinions, and expertise, demonstrate how a strong personal brand can lead to significant influence and financial opportunities. However, the commercialization of personal branding has also raised questions about authenticity, ethics, and the impact of social media on mental health and self-esteem.

Chapter 19: Social Media Trends: Fads that Fizzled

Social media trends have a dynamic and transient nature, often emerging explosively and capturing global attention before fading into obscurity just as rapidly. The lifecycle of these trends can offer insightful glimpses into the collective behaviors and interests of online communities. While some trends have staying power and significantly influence cultural or social norms, many others fizzle out, leaving behind only brief memories of their intense, if fleeting, popularity. Understanding these transient trends involves examining the factors that contribute to their rise and fall, the impact they have during their peak, and the reasons they eventually lose traction.

One of the most notorious fads that fizzled is the Harlem Shake phenomenon. In early 2013, this trend involved people creating videos that started with a single person dancing to the song "Harlem Shake" by Baauer, often in a restrained or unassuming manner, followed by a sudden cut to a chaotic scene where a group of people joined in, dancing wildly in costumes or using props. The format of these videos was simple, making it easy for anyone to participate, which fueled its rapid spread. Thousands of Harlem Shake videos were uploaded within a short span, and the trend even permeated mainstream media and corporate environments. Despite its explosive popularity, the Harlem Shake quickly faded as the novelty wore off and the internet's attention shifted elsewhere. The abrupt rise and fall of the Harlem Shake exemplify how social media trends can peak rapidly when they are easy to replicate and share but also how they can just as swiftly decline once they saturate the market.

Another example is the Ice Bucket Challenge, which took social media by storm in the summer of 2014. The challenge involved people pouring a bucket of ice water over their heads and nominating others to do the same, all while encouraging donations to amyotrophic lateral sclerosis (ALS) research. This trend was unique because it combined a viral challenge with a philanthropic cause, leading to widespread participation from celebrities, politicians, and ordinary individuals alike. The Ice Bucket Challenge raised over $115 million for ALS research, demonstrating the potential for social media trends to effect positive change. However, the challenge's intense popularity was short-lived. Once the initial wave of participation subsided and the novelty wore off, the trend disappeared from the social media landscape, leaving behind a significant, though momentary, impact on public awareness and charitable giving.

Planking is another social media fad that fizzled out. In 2011, planking involved people lying face down in unusual or public places, with their arms at their sides, and then sharing photos of their exploits online. The absurdity and simplicity of the act, combined with the potential for creativity in choosing plank locations, drove its initial popularity. However, as with many viral trends, planking's appeal was largely based on its novelty. Once the initial excitement waned and incidents of people taking dangerous risks to achieve more extreme planking photos emerged, the trend quickly lost its charm and faded away. The planking fad highlights how social media trends often thrive on the balance between novelty and participation but can quickly fizzle out if they become repetitive or hazardous.

The Mannequin Challenge, which surfaced in late 2016, is another illustrative example. This trend involved groups of people freezing in place like mannequins while a camera moved around them, typically set to the song "Black Beatles" by Rae Sremmurd. The challenge's appeal lay in its simplicity and the visual impact of large groups of people perfectly still, creating a tableau effect. Schools, sports teams, and celebrities participated, leading to a flood of mannequin challenge videos across social media platforms. However, like many trends driven by a specific format, the Mannequin Challenge quickly reached a saturation point where it became difficult to create fresh or engaging content. As a result, the trend fizzled out within a few months, showcasing how social media trends can rapidly lose momentum once they become overexposed.

Pokemon Go, while primarily a mobile game, also became a significant social media trend in the summer of 2016. The augmented reality game, which allowed players to catch virtual Pokemon in real-world locations, created a global sensation. Social media was flooded with stories, tips, and screenshots from players, and the game was credited with encouraging people to explore their surroundings and interact with others. Despite its initial explosive success, with millions of downloads and widespread media coverage, interest in Pokemon Go declined as the novelty wore off, technical issues arose, and players grew frustrated with the game's limitations. Although it retains a dedicated player base, the intense social media buzz that surrounded its launch has long since faded, exemplifying how even highly innovative and initially engaging trends can lose their luster over time.

The rise and fall of these trends underscore several common factors that contribute to their lifecycle. Novelty and ease of participation are critical in the early stages, as they drive widespread engagement and sharing. The social aspect, where people feel connected by participating in a collective experience, also plays a significant role. However, these same factors can lead to a trend's downfall. Once the novelty fades and the market becomes saturated, interest wanes. Additionally, trends that rely on a specific format or gimmick can struggle to sustain long-term engagement as content becomes repetitive.

The speed at which information spreads on social media also accelerates the lifecycle of trends. What once might have taken weeks or months to gain momentum can now happen in days or even hours, leading to a more rapid decline as well. The constant influx of new content means that attention spans are short, and users quickly move on to the next big thing.

The impact of social media trends, even those that fizzle out, should not be underestimated. During their peak, these trends can generate significant engagement, drive conversations, and even lead to real-world actions, such as charitable donations or increased physical activity. They can also provide valuable insights into collective behavior, preferences, and the social dynamics of online communities.

Chapter 20: Authenticity Online

In the vast and ever-evolving landscape of the internet, authenticity has emerged as a paramount value, one that resonates deeply with users seeking genuine connections and trustworthy information. The concept of authenticity online pertains to the representation of oneself, or one's brand, in a manner that is truthful, consistent, and reflective of real values and beliefs. As social media and digital platforms continue to dominate how we interact, work, and live, the quest for authenticity has become a central theme in discussions about digital identity, social influence, and online behavior.

The allure of authenticity stems from the intrinsic human desire for genuine interactions and relationships. In a digital world where images can be filtered, experiences can be curated, and personas can be meticulously crafted, distinguishing between what is real and what is fabricated can be challenging. Authenticity online, therefore, involves presenting oneself in a manner that is honest and transparent, avoiding the temptation to portray a falsely idealized version of reality.

One of the key challenges to maintaining authenticity online is the pressure to conform to societal expectations and the perceived standards of various online communities. Social media platforms, in particular, are rife with comparisons. Users often find themselves measuring their lives against the highlight reels of others, leading to a culture of perfectionism and superficiality. This environment can incentivize inauthentic behavior, as individuals may feel compelled to present themselves in ways that garner more likes, followers, or positive feedback, rather than in ways that are true to themselves.

Despite these pressures, many individuals and brands are increasingly prioritizing authenticity. For individuals, being authentic online means sharing not just successes and happy moments, but also challenges, failures, and everyday experiences. It involves using one's voice to express genuine opinions and emotions, rather than simply echoing popular sentiments. This kind of transparency can foster deeper connections and build a community of followers who appreciate and relate to the authenticity of the content being shared.

For brands, authenticity is about aligning their online presence with their core values and mission. It involves being honest about their products or services, admitting mistakes, and engaging with their audience in a sincere and human manner. Brands that embrace authenticity can build stronger, more loyal customer bases, as consumers are increasingly drawn to companies that they perceive as genuine and trustworthy. Authenticity in branding also means staying true to the brand's identity, rather than jumping on every trend or trying to appeal to every possible audience.

One significant aspect of authenticity online is the use of storytelling. Sharing personal stories, whether they are about everyday life or significant life events, can humanize an online presence and make it more relatable. Storytelling allows individuals and brands to connect with their audience on a deeper emotional level, fostering empathy and understanding. Authentic storytelling involves being vulnerable and open, revealing the real, unpolished aspects of one's life or journey.

Another important factor is consistency. Authenticity is not just about being truthful in individual posts or interactions but about maintaining a consistent representation of oneself over time. This consistency helps to build trust, as followers and audiences come to know what to expect and can rely on the authenticity of the content being shared. Inconsistent behavior, such as drastic changes in tone, style, or messaging, can lead to skepticism and erode the trust that has been built.

The rise of influencer culture has brought authenticity to the forefront of online discussions. Influencers, who build their careers on their online personas, are particularly scrutinized for their authenticity. Audiences can quickly detect when influencers are promoting products or lifestyles that do not align with their usual content or values, leading to accusations of inauthenticity. Successful influencers often strike a balance between sponsored content and genuine, unscripted posts, maintaining transparency about their partnerships and staying true to their personal brand.

However, the pursuit of authenticity is not without its complexities. The very act of trying to be authentic can sometimes feel performative, as individuals and brands navigate the fine line between being genuine and being perceived as genuine. The concept of "strategic authenticity" emerges in this context, where authenticity itself becomes a strategy for building credibility and trust. While this approach can be effective, it raises questions about the nature of authenticity and whether it can be truly genuine if it is being strategically crafted.

Moreover, cultural and social factors play a significant role in how authenticity is perceived and valued. What is considered authentic in one cultural context may not be viewed the same way in another. Understanding these nuances is important for individuals and brands operating in a global digital space. Being culturally sensitive and aware can enhance the authenticity of online interactions and communications.

The impact of technology on authenticity is another critical consideration. Advances in artificial intelligence, augmented reality, and virtual reality are transforming how we experience and interact with digital content. These technologies can blur the lines between what is real and what is artificial, presenting new challenges and opportunities for authenticity. For example, AI-generated content or deepfakes can create highly realistic but entirely fabricated personas or experiences, making it even more difficult to discern authenticity. On the other hand, these technologies can also be used to create more immersive and genuine experiences, enhancing the authenticity of virtual interactions.

Privacy and data security are also intertwined with the concept of authenticity online. Being authentic often involves sharing personal information and experiences, which can expose individuals to risks related to privacy breaches and data misuse. Balancing openness with the need to protect one's privacy is a delicate act. This balance is crucial for maintaining both authenticity and security in the digital realm.

The rise of social movements and activism on digital platforms highlights another dimension of authenticity online. Movements such as #MeToo, Black Lives Matter, and climate activism have leveraged the power of social media to amplify authentic voices and stories, driving significant social change. Authenticity in this context involves using one's platform to speak out on important issues, share personal experiences, and support causes in a genuine and consistent manner. However, it also requires vigilance against performative activism, where individuals or brands engage with social causes superficially for the sake of appearance rather than genuine commitment.

Educational and professional contexts are not immune to the pressures and benefits of authenticity online. Students, educators, and professionals increasingly use digital platforms to showcase their work, connect with peers, and build their careers. Authenticity in these contexts involves presenting one's achievements and skills truthfully, acknowledging both strengths and areas for improvement, and engaging in meaningful professional interactions. For educators, authenticity can also mean embracing new teaching methods and technologies while staying true to their pedagogical values and personal teaching style.

Chapter 21: The Algorithm Game: Playing to Win

In the realm of digital media, the concept of "The Algorithm Game" encapsulates the strategies and tactics employed by individuals, brands, and content creators to navigate and exploit the algorithms that govern the visibility and dissemination of content on social media platforms. Algorithms, the complex sets of rules and data processing sequences used by platforms like Facebook, Instagram, Twitter, YouTube, and TikTok, are designed to curate content for users based on their preferences, behaviors, and interactions. Understanding and playing the algorithm game effectively can significantly enhance one's online presence, engagement, and influence. However, this game is both intricate and ever-evolving, requiring constant adaptation and a deep understanding of digital ecosystems.

Algorithms primarily aim to enhance user experience by presenting content that is most relevant and engaging. They analyze a vast array of data points, including user interactions, likes, shares, comments, watch time, and even the time-of-day content is posted. By doing so, they create personalized feeds that keep users engaged longer, thereby increasing ad revenue for the platforms. However, for content creators, this presents both an opportunity and a challenge: how to craft content that algorithms favor while staying true to their message and audience.

One of the fundamental aspects of the algorithm game is understanding the specific ranking signals that each platform's algorithm considers important. On Facebook, for instance, the algorithm prioritizes content that fosters meaningful interactions. Posts that generate longer comments and encourage discussions are more likely to appear in users' feeds. On Instagram, the algorithm emphasizes engagement rates, favoring posts with higher likes, comments, and shares, as well as those that keep users on the platform longer, such as Stories and IGTV videos. YouTube's algorithm, on the other hand, prioritizes watch time and viewer retention, rewarding videos that keep viewers engaged for extended periods and lead them to watch more content.

Creating content that aligns with these ranking signals is essential. High-quality, engaging content that resonates with the audience is more likely to trigger positive algorithmic responses. This involves understanding what type of content your audience finds valuable and engaging. For instance, educational content, how-to videos, or emotionally resonant stories often perform well because they provide value and provoke reactions. Regularly analyzing metrics and feedback can provide insights into what works and what doesn't, allowing creators to refine their strategies continuously.

Consistency is another critical factor in the algorithm game. Most social media algorithms reward consistent posting schedules. For example, YouTube channels that post regularly are often favored by the algorithm, as consistent uploads encourage repeat visits from subscribers and increase overall watch time. Similarly, Instagram and TikTok algorithms tend to boost accounts that post frequently and consistently. This consistency helps build a reliable presence, making it easier for the algorithm to identify and promote your content.

Engagement with the audience is also pivotal. Responding to comments, liking replies, and engaging with followers can boost a post's visibility. These interactions signal to the algorithm that the content is generating meaningful engagement. Live sessions, Q&A formats, and interactive content like polls or quizzes can further enhance engagement rates. Additionally, fostering a community around your content encourages more interaction, which algorithms tend to favor.

The use of hashtags, keywords, and tags can significantly influence algorithmic outcomes. On platforms like Instagram and Twitter, hashtags help categorize content, making it discoverable to users interested in those topics. Effective use of trending and relevant hashtags can increase a post's reach beyond the creator's immediate followers. On YouTube, keywords and tags play a crucial role in search engine optimization (SEO), helping videos appear in search results and recommended feeds. Crafting descriptive, keyword-rich titles and descriptions can enhance discoverability.

Another aspect of the algorithm game is staying updated with platform changes and trends. Social media platforms frequently update their algorithms and features, impacting how content is ranked and displayed. Keeping abreast of these changes is crucial for adapting strategies. For instance, the introduction of Instagram Reels, a feature to compete with TikTok, prompted many creators to shift their content strategies to include short, engaging video clips. Similarly, YouTube's algorithm updates have increasingly prioritized viewer satisfaction metrics, leading creators to focus more on content quality and audience retention.

Leveraging multiple platforms can also be advantageous. Diversifying content distribution across various social media platforms mitigates the risk associated with algorithm changes on a single platform. It also broadens reach and engagement opportunities. For example, a content creator might use YouTube for long-form content, Instagram for visual storytelling, Twitter for real-time updates, and TikTok for short, viral videos. Each platform's unique algorithm and audience can amplify the overall impact of the content.

Collaborations and cross-promotions can further enhance algorithmic favorability. Partnering with other creators or brands can introduce content to new audiences and generate cross-platform engagement. For instance, collaborative videos or social media takeovers can attract followers from both parties, boosting visibility and engagement. These collaborations often lead to higher interaction rates, as audiences are drawn to the novelty and diversity of content.

Paid promotions and advertisements are another dimension of the algorithm game. Most social media platforms offer advertising options that can amplify content reach. While organic reach is valuable, strategically investing in paid promotions can ensure content reaches a broader and more targeted audience. Understanding how to effectively use these advertising tools, such as targeting specific demographics or utilizing A/B testing, can significantly enhance engagement and visibility.

However, the algorithm game is not without its criticisms and ethical considerations. The pressure to conform to algorithmic preferences can lead to content homogenization, where creators produce similar types of content to maximize engagement, potentially stifling creativity and diversity. Moreover, the focus on engagement metrics can incentivize sensationalism or clickbait tactics, leading to the spread of misleading or low-quality content.

The ethical implications extend to data privacy concerns. Algorithms rely on extensive data collection to function effectively, raising issues about user consent and the handling of personal information. The opaque nature of algorithms also means that users and creators often lack a clear understanding of how their data is used and how content is prioritized, leading to calls for greater transparency and accountability from social media companies.

Despite these challenges, playing the algorithm game effectively can lead to significant rewards. For individual creators, it can mean increased visibility, engagement, and monetization opportunities. For brands, it translates to better market reach, customer engagement, and ultimately, sales. The key lies in balancing algorithmic optimization with authenticity, creativity, and ethical considerations.

Chapter 22: Digital Relationships: Friends, Followers, and Foes

In today's interconnected world, digital relationships have become an integral part of our social fabric, shaping how we interact, communicate, and perceive each other. These relationships, formed and maintained through various online platforms, range from friendships and followers to more antagonistic interactions with so-called foes. The complexity and nuances of digital relationships reflect the broader human experience, with unique challenges and opportunities inherent to the digital realm. Understanding these relationships requires a deep dive into the dynamics of online interactions, the platforms that facilitate them, and the psychological and social impacts they engender.

Digital friendships often begin in much the same way as traditional ones: through common interests, shared experiences, and mutual connections. However, the digital environment allows for the formation of friendships across geographical boundaries, cultural differences, and time zones. Social media platforms like Facebook, Instagram, Twitter, and Snapchat provide the infrastructure for people to connect, share their lives, and maintain ongoing communication regardless of physical distance. These platforms offer various tools for interaction, including messaging, commenting, sharing posts, and even video chatting, which can foster a sense of closeness and intimacy.

One of the most profound impacts of digital friendships is the ability to maintain relationships over long distances and time periods. College friends, family members, and acquaintances can remain connected through regular updates and interactions online. This constant connectivity can strengthen bonds and provide a support system that might not be as readily available in the physical world. For example, during significant life events such as weddings, births, or even crises, friends can offer immediate support and celebrate milestones, thereby maintaining a sense of presence and solidarity.

However, digital friendships also face unique challenges. The absence of physical presence can lead to misunderstandings, as non-verbal cues such as tone of voice, facial expressions, and body language are often lost in text-based communication. Misinterpretations can occur, potentially leading to conflicts that might not arise in face-to-face interactions. Moreover, the curated nature of social media profiles can present an idealized version of oneself, which can sometimes lead to unrealistic expectations or feelings of inadequacy among friends. The phenomenon of "social media envy" arises when individuals compare their lives to the seemingly perfect lives of their friends, which can strain relationships and impact mental health.

Followers, particularly in the context of platforms like Instagram, Twitter, and TikTok, represent a different type of digital relationship. Followers can range from casual acquaintances to dedicated fans who engage with and support an individual's online persona. The dynamics of these relationships are often asymmetrical; while the content creator shares aspects of their life, followers consume and interact with this content, often without a reciprocal relationship. This dynamic can create a sense of connection and community among followers, who may feel a part of the creator's journey, celebrating their successes and sympathizing with their struggles.

For influencers and content creators, followers are crucial to their online presence and success. The number of followers can directly impact visibility, engagement, and monetization opportunities. Engaging with followers through comments, live sessions, and direct messages can foster a loyal community, which in turn can amplify the creator's reach and influence. However, the pressure to maintain a growing follower base can lead to content creators prioritizing engagement metrics over authenticity, sometimes resulting in burnout or the sacrifice of personal boundaries.

The relationship between content creators and followers also highlights the phenomenon of parasocial relationships, where followers develop a sense of intimacy and familiarity with a creator despite the relationship being one-sided. These relationships can be beneficial, providing followers with a sense of companionship and inspiration. However, they can also lead to unrealistic expectations or feelings of entitlement, where followers expect constant access or personal attention from the creator. Balancing the demands of a large follower base while maintaining personal well-being and authenticity is a complex challenge for many content creators.

On the other end of the spectrum are digital foes, or individuals with whom one has antagonistic relationships online. These relationships can arise from disagreements, conflicting beliefs, or simply the anonymity and distance afforded by the internet, which can embolden hostile behavior. Online trolling, cyberbullying, and harassment are manifestations of these antagonistic interactions. Platforms like Twitter, Reddit, and YouTube, where anonymity and public discourse are prevalent, often see higher instances of such negative interactions.

Cyberbullying and online harassment can have severe psychological impacts, including anxiety, depression, and in extreme cases, suicidal thoughts. The persistent and pervasive nature of digital communication means that victims can feel they have no respite from their tormentors. Moreover, the viral potential of social media can amplify harassment, leading to public shaming or doxxing (the release of private information online), which can have real-world consequences.

Addressing these negative interactions requires a multi-faceted approach, including platform policies, technological solutions, and societal changes. Social media companies have implemented various measures to combat online harassment, such as reporting mechanisms, automated content moderation, and stricter community guidelines. However, the effectiveness of these measures is often debated, as the sheer volume of content and the nuances of human interaction can make it challenging to enforce rules consistently.

Psychologically, the impact of digital relationships is profound. The constant connectivity and instant communication of the digital world can create a sense of immediacy and urgency, affecting how we process emotions and interact with others. Positive interactions and supportive communities can enhance well-being, providing a sense of belonging and connection. Conversely, negative interactions can exacerbate feelings of loneliness and isolation, especially when individuals face rejection or hostility online.

The concept of digital empathy is emerging as a crucial skill in navigating online relationships. Digital empathy involves understanding and responding to the emotions of others in online interactions, recognizing the humanity behind the screen. Promoting digital empathy can help mitigate conflicts and foster more supportive and constructive online communities. Educational initiatives and digital literacy programs that teach empathy and respectful communication can play a significant role in cultivating a healthier digital environment.

Moreover, the digital world blurs the boundaries between different types of relationships. Professional and personal lives often intersect online, as colleagues become Facebook friends, and LinkedIn connections turn into real-life acquaintances. This intersection can enrich relationships by providing deeper insights into each other's lives, but it can also create complexities in maintaining professional boundaries and managing different social roles.

Privacy and data security are critical considerations in digital relationships. The information we share online, whether through social media posts, messages, or interactions, is often stored and analyzed by platforms, raising concerns about data privacy. Understanding how to protect personal information and navigate privacy settings is essential for maintaining control over one's digital footprint. Additionally, being mindful of what and how much to share can help safeguard personal boundaries and reduce the risk of negative interactions.

Chapter 23: Selfies and Self-Worth: The Quest for Validation

In the age of social media, selfies have become a ubiquitous form of self-expression and communication. A selfie, typically a photograph taken by oneself using a smartphone or webcam, is often shared on social media platforms like Instagram, Facebook, Snapchat, and TikTok. While the act of taking selfies can be seen as a harmless, even empowering, way to capture moments and express oneself, it also intersects deeply with issues of self-worth and the quest for validation. The relationship between selfies and self-worth is complex and multifaceted, touching on psychological, social, and cultural dimensions.

The rise of selfies has fundamentally transformed how individuals perceive and present themselves. The immediacy and accessibility of smartphones allow people to document and share their lives in real-time. This constant connectivity and visibility can create an environment where individuals are perpetually seeking approval and validation from their online audiences. Likes, comments, shares, and followers become metrics by which people measure their self-worth and social standing. This phenomenon is particularly pronounced among younger generations who have grown up with social media as a central part of their lives.

The quest for validation through selfies often begins with the desire for positive reinforcement. When people post selfies, they are seeking affirmation of their appearance, experiences, and, by extension, their identities. Positive feedback in the form of likes and comments can boost self-esteem and provide a temporary sense of satisfaction and happiness. This reinforcement can be addictive, leading individuals to continuously seek out more approval through subsequent posts. The dopamine rush associated with receiving positive social media feedback is similar to the effects of other rewarding activities, reinforcing the behavior.

However, the pursuit of validation through selfies can also have detrimental effects on self-worth. The pressure to present a curated and idealized version of oneself can lead to feelings of inadequacy and anxiety. Comparing oneself to the seemingly perfect lives and appearances of others on social media can exacerbate these feelings, creating a cycle of negative self-assessment. This comparison culture, fueled by the proliferation of highly edited and filtered images, can distort perceptions of reality and beauty standards.

The use of filters and photo-editing apps has become a common practice in selfie culture. These tools allow users to enhance their appearance by smoothing skin, altering facial features, and even changing body shapes. While this can be fun and creative, it also sets unrealistic standards of beauty that are unattainable without digital manipulation. For many, the pressure to conform to these standards can lead to body dissatisfaction and a diminished sense of self-worth. The discrepancy between one's real appearance and their edited selfies can create a disconnect, leading to internal conflict and dissatisfaction.

Moreover, the focus on physical appearance in selfie culture can overshadow other aspects of identity and self-worth. The emphasis on looks can trivialize personal achievements, talents, and characteristics that are not as easily captured in a photograph. This reductionist view of self-worth, based primarily on appearance, can limit individuals' perceptions of their value and potential.

The impact of selfie culture on self-worth is not uniform and can vary based on individual differences and social contexts. For some, selfies can serve as a powerful tool for self-expression and empowerment. They can challenge traditional beauty standards by celebrating diverse appearances and identities. For instance, body positivity movements and campaigns promoting natural beauty often use selfies to spread their messages. These movements can empower individuals to embrace their uniqueness and find validation within supportive online communities.

However, the potential for negative effects remains significant, especially for those who are more vulnerable to social comparison and external validation. Adolescents and young adults, in particular, are at a critical stage of identity formation and are more susceptible to peer influence and social pressure. The feedback they receive on social media can significantly impact their self-esteem and self-worth. Negative comments, cyberbullying, and social rejection can have profound psychological effects, leading to issues such as depression, anxiety, and even eating disorders.

The role of social media influencers in shaping selfie culture and its impact on self-worth cannot be overlooked. Influencers often portray aspirational lifestyles and appearances, setting trends and standards that followers strive to emulate. While some influencers promote positive messages and realistic portrayals, many present highly curated and idealized versions of their lives. The commercial aspect of influencer culture, driven by sponsorships and advertising, can further perpetuate unrealistic standards as influencers are incentivized to maintain a certain image to attract brands and followers.

To mitigate the negative impact of selfies on self-worth, it is essential to foster a healthier and more balanced approach to social media use. Encouraging digital literacy and critical thinking skills can help individuals discern the reality behind the images they see and recognize the curated nature of social media content. Promoting authenticity and diverse representations can also challenge narrow beauty standards and provide a more inclusive view of self-worth.

Parents, educators, and mental health professionals play a crucial role in supporting individuals, particularly young people, in navigating the complexities of selfie culture. Open conversations about self-esteem, body image, and the pressures of social media can provide valuable support and guidance. Encouraging offline activities and relationships that promote a sense of achievement and connection can also help individuals build a more robust and multifaceted sense of self-worth.

Social media platforms themselves can contribute to healthier online environments by implementing features that promote positive interactions and reduce the emphasis on appearance-based validation. For example, Instagram's experiment with hiding likes aimed to reduce social pressure and encourage more authentic sharing. Continued efforts to enhance user well-being through platform design and policies can play a significant role in shaping the impact of selfie culture.

Chapter 24: Social Media and Politics

Social media has revolutionized the way politics is conducted, discussed, and perceived. It has transformed political communication, providing a platform for direct interaction between politicians and the public, enabling the rapid dissemination of information, and facilitating grassroots mobilization. However, the influence of social media on politics also comes with significant concerns about manipulation, misinformation, and the erosion of democratic processes. The multifaceted relationship between social media and politics encompasses a range of dynamics, from the empowerment of citizens and politicians alike to the exploitation of these platforms by malicious actors seeking to manipulate public opinion and disrupt political stability.

One of the most significant impacts of social media on politics is the democratization of information. Platforms like Facebook, Twitter, and Instagram allow politicians to communicate directly with constituents without the mediation of traditional news outlets. This direct line of communication can enhance transparency and accountability, as politicians can share their policies, respond to criticisms, and engage with the public in real-time. For example, former U.S. President Barack Obama's use of social media in his 2008 and 2012 campaigns was groundbreaking, leveraging these platforms to mobilize young voters, raise funds, and spread campaign messages efficiently.

Social media also enables the rapid dissemination of information, allowing political messages to reach a vast audience almost instantaneously. This speed and reach can be advantageous for raising awareness about issues, rallying support for causes, and coordinating political movements. The Arab Spring, a series of anti-government protests and uprisings in the early 2010s, is a notable example of social media's power to facilitate political change. Platforms like Twitter and

Facebook played crucial roles in organizing protests, sharing information, and galvanizing international support, demonstrating how social media can be a tool for empowerment and democratic participation.

Grassroots mobilization is another critical aspect of social media's influence on politics. Activists and political organizations use these platforms to build communities, organize events, and engage supporters. Hashtags, viral videos, and online petitions are tools that can amplify voices and drive political action. Movements such as Black Lives Matter and #MeToo have leveraged social media to bring attention to systemic injustices, mobilize supporters globally, and pressure institutions to enact change. The ability to organize and mobilize quickly and effectively has made social media an indispensable tool for contemporary political activism.

However, the influence of social media on politics is not without its dark side. The same features that make these platforms powerful tools for communication and mobilization also make them vulnerable to manipulation and abuse. One of the most pressing concerns is the spread of misinformation and fake news. The viral nature of social media allows false information to spread rapidly, often outpacing efforts to verify and correct it. This can lead to widespread public misconceptions, undermine trust in legitimate news sources, and distort political discourse.

The 2016 U.S. presidential election is a case study in the impact of misinformation on social media. During the election, a significant amount of false and misleading information was disseminated on platforms like Facebook and Twitter. Some of this misinformation was propagated by domestic actors, while other sources were linked to foreign interference, particularly by Russian operatives aiming to sow discord and influence the election outcome. The proliferation of fake news created a polluted information environment, complicating voters' ability to make informed decisions and eroding trust in democratic institutions.

Social media algorithms also play a crucial role in shaping political discourse. These algorithms are designed to maximize user engagement by prioritizing content that is likely to elicit strong reactions, such as anger or outrage. This can lead to the amplification of sensationalist, polarizing, and extreme content, contributing to political polarization and the fragmentation of public discourse. The echo chamber effect, where users are predominantly exposed to information that reinforces their existing beliefs, can further entrench divisions and hinder constructive dialogue.

Manipulation of social media for political purposes extends beyond misinformation to more covert and sophisticated tactics. Botnets, networks of automated accounts, can artificially inflate the popularity of certain messages, create the illusion of consensus, and drown out dissenting voices. Coordinated campaigns by state and non-state actors can target specific demographics with tailored propaganda, exploiting social and political tensions to manipulate public opinion. These tactics undermine the integrity of democratic processes and can destabilize societies by exacerbating divisions and eroding trust in institutions.

Privacy and data exploitation are additional concerns in the context of social media and politics. Platforms collect vast amounts of data on users' behaviors, preferences, and interactions, which can be used for targeted political advertising. The Cambridge Analytica scandal, where the data of millions of Facebook users was harvested without consent for political advertising purposes, highlighted the potential for misuse of personal data. Such practices raise ethical questions about consent, transparency, and the manipulation of voters through micro-targeting techniques that exploit psychological vulnerabilities.

The role of social media companies in moderating content and curbing abuse is a contentious issue. These companies wield significant power over what information is disseminated and how it is prioritized, making them de facto gatekeepers of public discourse. Efforts to combat misinformation, hate speech, and manipulation through content moderation and fact-checking are essential but fraught with challenges. Balancing the need to protect free speech with the responsibility to prevent harm is a complex task, and social media companies often face criticism from all sides for either overstepping or failing to act sufficiently.

Regulation of social media in the political context is a topic of ongoing debate. Some argue that stronger regulations are necessary to protect democratic processes and ensure accountability, while others caution against measures that could stifle innovation and infringe on free speech. Transparency in political advertising, clearer guidelines on content moderation, and robust data protection laws are potential regulatory approaches that could mitigate some of the negative impacts of social media on politics.

The international dimension of social media and politics adds another layer of complexity. Global platforms operate across diverse political systems and cultural contexts, making it challenging to develop universal standards and practices. Moreover, state actors can use social media as tools of geopolitical influence, engaging in information warfare to achieve strategic objectives. The ability of foreign entities to interfere in domestic politics through social media underscores the need for international cooperation and norms to address these transnational challenges.

Chapter 25: The Art of Unplugging: Digital Minimalism

In an era where digital connectivity is pervasive, the art of unplugging and embracing digital minimalism has gained significant traction. Digital minimalism advocates for a deliberate and mindful approach to technology use, prioritizing meaningful interactions and engagements while minimizing distractions and the overuse of digital devices. This philosophy seeks to reclaim time, attention, and well-being from the constant demands of the digital world, promoting a healthier, more balanced relationship with technology. To fully appreciate the implications and benefits of digital minimalism, it is essential to explore its principles, practices, and the underlying reasons driving this movement.

The concept of digital minimalism is rooted in the broader philosophy of minimalism, which emphasizes simplicity and the intentional elimination of excess. Just as minimalism in physical spaces advocates for decluttering and focusing on what truly matters, digital minimalism encourages individuals to declutter their digital lives. This involves reducing unnecessary digital consumption, curating online experiences, and fostering more intentional and purposeful use of technology. Digital minimalism is not about rejecting technology altogether; rather, it is about harnessing its benefits while mitigating its negative impacts.

One of the core principles of digital minimalism is intentionality. This involves making conscious choices about when, how, and why to use digital devices and platforms. Rather than mindlessly scrolling through social media feeds or incessantly checking emails, digital minimalists set clear boundaries and intentions for their technology use. This might mean designating specific times for checking social media, turning off notifications, or scheduling tech-free periods during the day. By being intentional, individuals can reduce the cognitive load and stress associated with constant connectivity and reclaim their attention for more meaningful activities.

Another key aspect of digital minimalism is the focus on quality over quantity. In a digital world overflowing with content, it is easy to become overwhelmed by the sheer volume of information. Digital minimalists prioritize high-quality, meaningful interactions and content that align with their values and goals. This might involve curating social media feeds to include only positive and inspiring accounts, subscribing to a few high-quality newsletters instead of dozens of irrelevant ones, or limiting media consumption to trusted sources. By focusing on quality, individuals can cultivate a more enriching and fulfilling digital experience.

The practice of digital decluttering is a common starting point for those adopting digital minimalism. Digital decluttering involves systematically evaluating and reducing the digital clutter that accumulates over time. This can include deleting unused apps, organizing files and emails, unsubscribing from unnecessary newsletters, and cleaning up social media connections. The process of digital decluttering can be liberating, creating a sense of order and clarity in one's digital environment. It also serves as a foundation for more mindful and intentional technology use going forward.

A significant driver of the digital minimalism movement is the growing awareness of the negative impacts of excessive screen time on mental and physical well-being. Numerous studies have highlighted the links between heavy technology use and issues such as anxiety, depression, sleep disturbances, and reduced productivity. The constant influx of notifications, messages, and updates can create a state of perpetual distraction, making it difficult to focus and be present in the moment. Digital minimalism offers a remedy by promoting practices that reduce digital overload and foster greater mental clarity and peace.

The concept of "attention economy" is central to understanding the need for digital minimalism. The attention economy refers to the commodification of human attention, where various digital platforms and apps compete to capture and retain users' attention. Social media platforms, for example, are designed with features that encourage prolonged engagement, such as infinite scrolling, autoplay videos, and algorithm-driven content recommendations. These design elements exploit psychological triggers, making it challenging for users to disconnect and control their screen time. Digital minimalism advocates for reclaiming control over one's attention and resisting the manipulative tactics of the attention economy.

Digital minimalism also intersects with the pursuit of deeper, more meaningful human connections. While digital communication tools can facilitate connections, they often fall short of providing the depth and richness of face-to-face interactions. The overreliance on digital communication can lead to superficial relationships and a sense of isolation. Digital minimalists prioritize real-world interactions and invest in relationships that foster genuine connection and intimacy. This might involve setting aside time for in-person gatherings, engaging in meaningful conversations, and being fully present with loved ones without the distraction of digital devices.

The benefits of digital minimalism extend beyond individual well-being to encompass broader societal and environmental impacts. The production and disposal of digital devices have significant environmental costs, including resource depletion and electronic waste. By adopting digital minimalism, individuals can reduce their consumption of digital products, extend the lifespan of their devices, and minimize their environmental footprint. Moreover, a more mindful approach to technology can contribute to a culture that values sustainability and responsible consumption.

Implementing digital minimalism can take various forms, depending on individual preferences and circumstances. One common approach is the digital detox, a temporary period of complete disconnection from digital devices. Digital detoxes can range from a few hours to several days and are designed to reset one's relationship with technology. During a digital detox, individuals can engage in activities that do not involve screens, such as reading, hiking, spending time with family, or pursuing hobbies. The experience can provide valuable insights into one's digital habits and highlight the benefits of reduced screen time.

Another approach is the practice of setting specific boundaries and rules for technology use. This might include creating no-phone zones in the home, such as the bedroom or dining area, implementing tech-free times, such as during meals or before bedtime, and establishing limits on social media usage. By setting clear boundaries, individuals can create a healthier balance between digital and offline life, reducing the intrusion of technology into personal time and space.

Digital minimalism also encourages the cultivation of alternative, offline activities that provide fulfillment and joy. Engaging in hobbies, physical exercise, creative pursuits, and nature activities can offer a sense of satisfaction and well-being that digital interactions often cannot. These activities provide opportunities for mindfulness, creativity, and physical health, contributing to a more holistic and balanced lifestyle.

The journey toward digital minimalism is highly personal and may require experimentation and adjustment. It is essential to recognize that digital minimalism is not a one-size-fits-all solution; what works for one person may not be suitable for another. The goal is to find a sustainable and fulfilling balance that enhances one's quality of life. This process may involve trial and error, self-reflection, and a willingness to adapt and evolve one's approach over time.

Chapter 26: Social Media for Good

Social media, often criticized for its negative impacts on mental health, privacy, and misinformation, also has a powerful and transformative potential for good. When leveraged responsibly, social media platforms can act as catalysts for positive change, fostering connections, enhancing communication, and driving social, economic, and cultural advancements. The positive impacts and initiatives facilitated by social media are vast, ranging from amplifying social justice movements and democratizing information to supporting mental health and fostering global collaboration.

Social media's ability to connect individuals across the globe is one of its most profound benefits. Platforms like Facebook, Twitter, Instagram, and LinkedIn have transformed the way people communicate, enabling instant interactions that transcend geographical boundaries. This connectivity fosters a sense of global community, allowing people to share experiences, ideas, and cultures. For instance, during natural disasters or humanitarian crises, social media serves as a crucial tool for real-time communication, facilitating the coordination of relief efforts and enabling individuals to seek and offer help. The speed and reach of social media have proven invaluable in times of crisis, providing a platform for disseminating critical information quickly and efficiently.

Moreover, social media has become an essential tool for social activism and advocacy, amplifying voices that might otherwise go unheard. Movements like #BlackLivesMatter, #MeToo, and #ClimateStrike have harnessed the power of social media to raise awareness, mobilize supporters, and drive significant societal change. These platforms enable activists to reach a global audience, organize events, and apply pressure on policymakers. The viral nature of social media allows issues to gain traction rapidly, bringing them to the forefront of public discourse and fostering a collective sense of urgency for action.

In the realm of education and information dissemination, social media plays a pivotal role in democratizing access to knowledge. Educational institutions, organizations, and individuals use platforms like YouTube, Twitter, and Facebook to share educational content, tutorials, and lectures, making learning accessible to a broader audience. This democratization of information breaks down barriers to education, allowing people from diverse backgrounds to acquire new skills and knowledge, thereby fostering a more informed and educated society. Additionally, social media platforms serve as a hub for professional networking and career development. LinkedIn, for instance, connects professionals worldwide, offering opportunities for networking, job searching, and skill development. It enables individuals to showcase their expertise, connect with potential employers, and stay updated with industry trends.

Social media also plays a crucial role in promoting mental health awareness and providing support. Online communities and support groups offer a safe space for individuals to share their experiences, seek advice, and find comfort in knowing they are not alone in their struggles. Mental health professionals and organizations use social media to disseminate information, raise awareness about mental health issues, and provide resources and support. Campaigns like #BellLetsTalk and #MentalHealthAwareness harness the power of social media to reduce stigma, promote understanding, and encourage individuals to seek help.

In terms of economic impact, social media has transformed the landscape of business and marketing, providing a platform for entrepreneurs and small businesses to reach a wider audience. Social media platforms enable businesses to engage with customers, build brand loyalty, and market their products and services cost-effectively. The rise of social commerce allows businesses to sell directly to consumers through social media, streamlining the purchasing process and enhancing customer experience. Additionally, the influencer economy has created new opportunities for individuals to monetize their online presence and expertise, leading to the emergence of new career paths and revenue streams.

Social media's role in fostering cultural exchange and understanding is also significant. Platforms like Instagram, TikTok, and YouTube provide a space for individuals to share their cultural practices, traditions, and experiences, promoting cross-cultural understanding and appreciation. This exposure to diverse perspectives and ways of life helps to break down stereotypes and prejudices, fostering a more inclusive and empathetic global community. Social media campaigns that celebrate cultural diversity and advocate for social justice contribute to a more tolerant and accepting society.

Environmental awareness and advocacy have also benefited greatly from social media. Platforms provide a powerful tool for environmental activists to raise awareness about issues such as climate change, deforestation, and pollution. Campaigns like #FridaysForFuture and #PlasticFreeJuly have used social media to mobilize millions of individuals worldwide to take action for the environment. These initiatives leverage the reach and influence of social media to promote sustainable practices, advocate for policy changes, and encourage individual and collective action to protect the planet.

Furthermore, social media has played a critical role in political engagement and participation, empowering citizens to voice their opinions, engage in discussions, and participate in the democratic process. Platforms like Twitter and Facebook have become essential tools for political campaigns, allowing candidates to communicate directly with voters, share their platforms, and mobilize supporters. Social media also provides a platform for civic engagement, enabling individuals to advocate for causes they care about, participate in political discourse, and hold leaders accountable.

In addition to these broader societal impacts, social media has also enabled numerous specific initiatives that drive positive change. For example, the #GivingTuesday campaign leverages social media to encourage charitable giving and volunteerism, raising millions of dollars for nonprofit organizations worldwide. Similarly, crowdfunding platforms like GoFundMe and Kickstarter have used social media to raise funds for various causes, from medical expenses and disaster relief to innovative projects and startups. These initiatives demonstrate the power of social media to harness collective goodwill and drive positive outcomes.

Social media's role in fostering innovation and collaboration cannot be overstated. Platforms like LinkedIn and Twitter facilitate connections between professionals, researchers, and innovators, fostering collaboration and knowledge sharing. This has led to the development of new ideas, technologies, and solutions to global challenges. For instance, open-source projects and collaborative research initiatives have benefited from the connectivity and information sharing enabled by social media, driving advancements in fields such as technology, medicine, and environmental science.

Chapter 27: The Screen Time Dilemma

The screen time dilemma is a multifaceted issue that affects people of all ages in today's digital world. With the proliferation of smartphones, tablets, computers, and other digital devices, managing screen time has become a critical aspect of daily life. The challenge lies not only in understanding the implications of excessive screen use but also in developing effective strategies to manage it. This topic encompasses a broad spectrum of considerations, including health impacts, psychological effects, productivity concerns, social implications, and strategies for balanced usage.

At the heart of the screen time dilemma is the undeniable fact that digital devices are deeply integrated into our lives. They are indispensable for work, education, communication, and entertainment. However, the convenience and necessity of these devices often lead to excessive usage, which can have adverse effects on both physical and mental health. Prolonged screen time is linked to a range of health issues, including eye strain, poor posture, and disrupted sleep patterns. Digital Eye Strain (DES), also known as Computer Vision Syndrome, is a common condition characterized by symptoms such as dry eyes, headaches, blurred vision, and neck and shoulder pain. The blue light emitted by screens can interfere with the body's natural sleep-wake cycle, making it difficult to fall asleep and reducing the quality of sleep. This disruption in sleep can lead to a range of issues, including fatigue, decreased cognitive function, and an increased risk of mental health problems such as anxiety and depression.

Beyond the physical health implications, excessive screen time also poses significant psychological risks. The constant bombardment of information and stimuli from digital devices can lead to cognitive overload, reducing our ability to concentrate and process information effectively. This can result in a diminished attention span and increased difficulty in focusing on tasks, both of which are detrimental to productivity and overall cognitive health. Additionally, the pervasive nature of social media and digital communication can contribute to feelings of loneliness, anxiety, and depression. The pressure to maintain a certain image or lifestyle on social media can lead to negative self-comparisons and a sense of inadequacy, particularly among young people. The phenomenon of FOMO (Fear Of Missing Out) is exacerbated by social media, as users are constantly exposed to curated portrayals of others' lives, leading to anxiety and a sense of exclusion.

The impact of screen time on productivity is another critical aspect of the dilemma. While digital devices and the internet offer unparalleled access to information and tools that can enhance productivity, they also present numerous distractions that can hinder it. Notifications from social media, email, and other apps can interrupt workflow and reduce the amount of focused time spent on tasks. This constant state of distraction can lead to multitasking, which has been shown to reduce overall efficiency and the quality of work. The challenge lies in finding a balance between leveraging technology for productivity and avoiding the pitfalls of distraction and information overload.

Social implications of screen time are equally significant. The rise of digital communication has transformed the way we interact with others, offering both benefits and drawbacks. On one hand, technology allows us to stay connected with friends and family across distances, facilitating communication that would otherwise be difficult or impossible. On the other hand, the quality of these interactions can suffer. Digital communication often lacks the depth and nuance of face-to-face interactions, which can lead to misunderstandings and a reduced sense of social connection. Furthermore, excessive screen time can encroach on time that could be spent on physical activities, hobbies, or face-to-face socializing, potentially leading to social isolation and a sedentary lifestyle.

Given these challenges, managing screen time effectively is essential for maintaining a healthy and balanced life. The first step in addressing the screen time dilemma is to raise awareness of the issue and its potential impacts. Individuals need to understand how much time they are spending on their devices and how this time is being allocated. Many smartphones and computers now come with built-in tools that track screen time and provide insights into usage patterns. These tools can help individuals identify areas where they may be spending too much time and set goals for reducing usage.

Setting clear boundaries around screen time is another important strategy. This can include setting specific times of the day for checking email and social media, establishing a cut-off time for device use before bed, and designating certain areas of the home as screen-free zones. These boundaries can help to reduce the overall amount of time spent on screens and mitigate some of the negative effects associated with excessive use. Additionally, it is important to prioritize activities that do not involve screens, such as physical exercise, reading, or spending time with family and friends. These activities can provide a necessary break from screens and help to promote a more balanced and fulfilling lifestyle.

Creating a balanced screen time routine also involves making conscious choices about the content we consume. It is important to be mindful of the quality of content and to seek out information and entertainment that is enriching and meaningful. This can include setting limits on time spent on social media and other potentially addictive platforms and focusing instead on activities that contribute to personal growth and well-being. Educational content, hobbies, and skill development can offer more substantial benefits than passive consumption of entertainment and social media.

In addition to individual strategies, there is a growing need for societal and policy-level interventions to address the screen time dilemma. Schools, workplaces, and governments can play a crucial role in promoting healthy screen use. Educational institutions can incorporate digital literacy programs that teach students about the risks of excessive screen time and the importance of balancing screen use with other activities. Workplaces can implement policies that encourage regular breaks from screens and promote a healthy work-life balance. Governments can support research into the impacts of screen time and develop guidelines and regulations that promote responsible use of digital devices.

Technology companies also have a responsibility to design products that promote healthy usage patterns. This can include features that limit usage time, reduce the frequency of notifications, and provide options for more meaningful and less distracting interactions. Companies can also support initiatives that promote digital well-being and fund research into the impacts of their products on users' health and well-being.

Chapter 28: Online Etiquette: Manners in the Digital Age

In the ever-evolving landscape of the digital age, online etiquette, often referred to as "netiquette," has become an essential aspect of maintaining respectful, effective, and positive interactions across the myriad platforms that constitute the internet. As our personal and professional lives increasingly shift online, understanding and practicing good online manners are crucial for fostering a harmonious digital environment. The topic of online etiquette encompasses a wide range of behaviors and practices, including communication norms, privacy considerations, and the ethical use of digital resources. It is an expansive field that addresses how we conduct ourselves in emails, social media, forums, virtual meetings, and other online spaces. Here, we will explore the intricacies of online etiquette in detail, examining its significance, the challenges of maintaining civility in digital interactions, and the principles that guide proper behavior in the digital realm.

At its core, online etiquette is about respect and consideration for others in the digital space. Just as there are rules of behavior for in-person interactions, there are established norms and expectations for how we should behave online. However, the anonymity and physical distance provided by digital platforms can sometimes lead to a breakdown in these norms, resulting in negative behaviors such as cyberbullying, trolling, and the spread of misinformation. Understanding and adhering to online etiquette helps to mitigate these issues by promoting respectful and constructive interactions.

One of the most fundamental aspects of online etiquette is communication. Clear, respectful, and thoughtful communication is key to effective online interactions, whether through email, social media, or other digital platforms. When composing an email, for example, it is important to consider the tone, clarity, and content of the message. Emails should be concise and to the point, with a clear subject line that accurately reflects the content. It is also important to use appropriate greetings and sign-offs, and to avoid using all caps, which can be perceived as shouting. Additionally, one should be mindful of the recipient's time and avoid sending unnecessary or overly frequent emails.

In social media interactions, the principles of good communication extend to comments, posts, and messages. It is important to engage in respectful dialogue, even when discussing controversial or sensitive topics. This means avoiding inflammatory language, personal attacks, and unfounded accusations. Instead, individuals should strive to express their opinions thoughtfully and considerately, and to listen to and understand the perspectives of others. Social media also requires a level of awareness regarding the audience and the potential impact of one's words and actions. What might seem like a harmless comment to one person could be offensive or hurtful to another, so it is important to think before posting and to be mindful of the broader implications of one's online behavior.

Another critical component of online etiquette is the respect for privacy and confidentiality. The ease with which information can be shared and accessed online has made privacy a significant concern. It is essential to respect the privacy of others by not sharing personal information or images without their consent, and by being mindful of the security and confidentiality of information shared online. This includes understanding and respecting the privacy settings of social media platforms, and ensuring that sensitive information is not inadvertently shared with a wider audience than intended.

In addition to communication and privacy, online etiquette also involves the ethical use of digital resources. This includes respecting intellectual property rights by not plagiarizing content, properly attributing sources, and seeking permission before using someone else's work. It also involves being mindful of the bandwidth and digital resources one consumes, and not engaging in activities that could disrupt or harm the online experience of others, such as spamming, hacking, or distributing malware.

The rise of virtual meetings and remote work has also brought new considerations for online etiquette. In virtual meetings, it is important to be punctual, prepared, and to dress appropriately, just as one would for an in-person meeting. Participants should mute their microphones when not speaking to minimize background noise, use video when possible to facilitate a more personal connection, and avoid multitasking during the meeting. Additionally, it is important to respect the host's agenda and time constraints, and to participate actively and respectfully in the discussion.

One of the key challenges in maintaining online etiquette is the anonymity and distance provided by digital platforms. The lack of face-to-face interaction can sometimes lead to a phenomenon known as the "online disinhibition effect," where individuals feel less restrained and more likely to engage in negative behaviors than they would in person. This can lead to issues such as cyberbullying, trolling, and the spread of misinformation and hate speech. To counteract this, it is important to cultivate a sense of accountability and responsibility in online interactions. This means recognizing that there are real people behind the screens and that our words and actions can have significant impacts on others.

Another challenge is the diversity of online platforms and the varying norms and expectations associated with each. What might be considered acceptable behavior on one platform might not be appropriate on another. For example, the casual and informal tone that is common on social media platforms like Twitter or Instagram might not be suitable for a professional networking site like LinkedIn. It is important to understand and adhere to the specific norms and expectations of each platform, and to adapt one's behavior accordingly.

In addition to these challenges, the rapid pace of technological change and the constant evolution of digital platforms can make it difficult to keep up with the latest trends and best practices in online etiquette. What was considered appropriate behavior a few years ago may no longer be relevant or effective today. To navigate this dynamic landscape, it is important to stay informed and adaptable, and to be willing to learn and evolve one's approach to online interactions.

Despite these challenges, there are several principles that can guide good online etiquette across different platforms and contexts. One of the most important principles is the Golden Rule: "Treat others as you would like to be treated." This means showing respect, kindness, and consideration for others, and striving to create a positive and constructive online environment. Another important principle is to think before you post. This means taking a moment to consider the potential impact of your words and actions, and whether they are respectful, constructive, and appropriate for the context. It also means being mindful of the potential for misunderstanding or misinterpretation, and striving to communicate clearly and effectively.

Another key principle is to respect the diversity of the online community. The internet is a global platform that brings together people from a wide range of backgrounds, cultures, and perspectives. It is important to recognize and respect this diversity, and to be open to different viewpoints and ways of thinking. This means being mindful of cultural sensitivities, avoiding stereotypes and prejudices, and striving to foster an inclusive and respectful online environment.

Chapter 29: The Virtual You

The concept of the "virtual you," or digital identity, has become increasingly important in our interconnected world. With the proliferation of social media, professional networking sites, and various online platforms, managing one's digital identity is crucial for personal and professional success. A digital identity encompasses the persona you present online, which includes your activities, interactions, and the content you share. This digital footprint can significantly impact your reputation, relationships, and opportunities.

Creating a digital identity begins with understanding what it entails. At its core, a digital identity is the aggregation of your online presence, including social media profiles, professional accounts, blogs, forums, and any other digital interactions. It encompasses everything from your username and profile picture to the content you post and the way you interact with others online. This digital presence represents you in the virtual world, shaping how others perceive you. Just as your actions and words in the physical world contribute to your identity, your online activities contribute to your digital identity.

One of the primary components of a digital identity is your social media presence. Platforms like Facebook, Instagram, Twitter, LinkedIn, and TikTok allow users to create profiles, share content, and interact with others. Each platform serves a different purpose and audience, and the way you present yourself on each platform can vary significantly. For example, LinkedIn is geared towards professional networking, so your profile on this platform might emphasize your career achievements, skills, and professional interests. On the other hand, Instagram and TikTok are more focused on personal and creative expression, where you might share photos, videos, and stories that reflect your hobbies, interests, and personal life.

When creating a digital identity, it is important to consider how you want to be perceived by others. This involves curating your online presence in a way that aligns with your values, goals, and the image you wish to project. For instance, if you are an aspiring professional, you might want to highlight your expertise, experience, and accomplishments on platforms like LinkedIn and Twitter. On more personal platforms like Instagram or Facebook, you might choose to share aspects of your life that reflect your interests, hobbies, and personality. The key is to create a cohesive and authentic online persona that accurately represents who you are and what you stand for.

However, it is important to recognize that the image you project online is only part of your digital identity. Your online activities, including the comments you make, the content you share, and the interactions you have with others, also contribute to your digital footprint. This footprint can have lasting implications for your reputation and opportunities. For example, positive interactions and constructive contributions to online communities can enhance your reputation and open up new opportunities. Conversely, negative behavior, such as posting inappropriate content or engaging in online arguments, can damage your reputation and limit your opportunities.

The implications of a digital footprint are far-reaching and can impact various aspects of your life. For example, employers increasingly use social media and online searches to screen job candidates. A positive digital identity can enhance your chances of landing a job, while a negative online presence can disqualify you from consideration. Similarly, educational institutions often consider applicants' digital footprints as part of their admissions process. A well-maintained digital identity that reflects your academic achievements, extracurricular activities, and community involvement can improve your chances of being accepted into your desired program.

In addition to professional and educational implications, your digital identity can also affect your personal relationships and social interactions. The way you present yourself online can influence how others perceive you and how they interact with you. For example, sharing positive and uplifting content can attract like-minded individuals and foster meaningful connections, while sharing controversial or divisive content can lead to conflicts and damaged relationships. It is important to be mindful of the impact your online presence can have on your personal and social life, and to strive to maintain a positive and respectful digital identity.

Creating and maintaining a digital identity also involves understanding and managing the risks associated with an online presence. One of the most significant risks is the potential for identity theft and privacy breaches. Personal information shared online can be exploited by malicious actors for various purposes, including financial fraud, identity theft, and cyberbullying. To protect yourself, it is important to be cautious about the information you share online and to use strong, unique passwords for your accounts. Additionally, it is important to be aware of the privacy settings on the platforms you use and to adjust them to control who can see your information and what they can access.

Another risk associated with a digital identity is the potential for online harassment and cyberbullying. The anonymity and distance provided by the internet can embolden individuals to engage in negative behaviors that they might not engage in face-to-face. This can lead to harmful interactions that can damage your reputation, mental health, and overall well-being. To mitigate this risk, it is important to be mindful of the content you share and the interactions you have online, and to use tools and resources available on digital platforms to report and block abusive behavior.

In addition to these risks, it is also important to be aware of the potential for digital addiction and over-reliance on online validation. The constant need to check notifications, post updates, and seek approval from others can lead to unhealthy habits and negatively impact your mental health and well-being. To maintain a healthy balance, it is important to set boundaries around your online activities and to prioritize offline relationships and activities that contribute to your overall well-being.

Maintaining a positive and coherent digital identity requires ongoing effort and attention. This involves regularly reviewing and updating your online profiles to ensure that they accurately reflect your current interests, achievements, and goals. It also involves being mindful of the content you share and the interactions you have online, and striving to project a positive and respectful image in all your digital interactions.

One effective strategy for maintaining a positive digital identity is to regularly audit your online presence. This involves searching for your name online to see what information is available about you, and reviewing your social media profiles and other online accounts to ensure that they accurately reflect the image you want to project. If you find any content that is outdated, inaccurate, or unflattering, take steps to remove or update it. This can help to ensure that your digital identity remains consistent and positive.

Another important aspect of maintaining a digital identity is to be mindful of your digital footprint and to take steps to protect your privacy and security. This includes using strong, unique passwords for your accounts, being cautious about the information you share online, and regularly reviewing and adjusting your privacy settings. It is also important to be aware of the potential for identity theft and other online risks, and to take steps to protect yourself, such as using two-factor authentication and being cautious about the links and attachments you open.

In addition to these practical steps, it is also important to cultivate a positive and respectful online presence. This involves being mindful of the content you share and the interactions you have online, and striving to contribute positively to the online communities you are a part of. By projecting a positive and respectful image, you can build a digital identity that reflects your values and enhances your reputation and opportunities.

Chapter 30: The Instant Gratification Trap

The phenomenon of instant gratification, characterized by the desire for immediate rewards or satisfaction, has become increasingly prevalent in our fast-paced, technology-driven world. This concept, often referred to as the "instant gratification trap," has significant implications for various aspects of our lives, including personal development, relationships, mental health, and overall well-being. The modern era, marked by rapid technological advancements and the availability of information and services at our fingertips, has exacerbated our natural inclination towards instant gratification.

Instant gratification is deeply rooted in human psychology and can be traced back to our evolutionary past. Our ancestors, living in environments where resources were scarce and survival was uncertain, had to seize opportunities for immediate rewards, such as food and shelter, to ensure their survival. This tendency for immediate reward-seeking is embedded in our brain's reward system, primarily regulated by the neurotransmitter dopamine. When we receive a reward, dopamine is released, creating a feeling of pleasure and reinforcing behaviors that lead to similar rewards in the future. This mechanism, which served our ancestors well in a world of immediate survival needs, has become maladaptive in our contemporary society, where many rewards are readily available and the consequences of impulsive behaviors are less immediate but potentially more harmful.

In today's world, technology plays a central role in facilitating instant gratification. The internet, smartphones, and social media platforms provide us with immediate access to information, entertainment, and social interaction. With just a few clicks or taps, we can satisfy our cravings for knowledge, amusement, and social connection. Online shopping allows us to purchase goods and have them delivered to our doorstep within hours or days. Streaming services enable us to watch movies and TV shows on demand, without the need to wait for scheduled broadcasts. Social media platforms provide instant validation through likes, comments, and shares. These conveniences, while undoubtedly beneficial in many ways, have also conditioned us to expect immediate satisfaction in all areas of our lives, leading to a diminished capacity for patience and long-term thinking.

The instant gratification trap has significant implications for personal development and goal attainment. Achieving meaningful goals and making significant life changes typically require sustained effort, discipline, and patience. However, the allure of immediate rewards can divert our attention and energy away from these long-term pursuits. For instance, a student who succumbs to the temptation of social media distractions may struggle to focus on their studies, leading to poorer academic performance. An individual who opts for the immediate pleasure of unhealthy snacks over a balanced diet may undermine their long-term health goals. The tendency to prioritize short-term rewards over long-term benefits can hinder personal growth, limit our potential, and contribute to feelings of frustration and dissatisfaction.

Moreover, the instant gratification trap can have profound effects on mental health. The constant pursuit of immediate satisfaction can lead to a cycle of dependency on quick fixes, such as binge-watching, online shopping, or social media engagement, as a means of coping with stress or boredom. This can result in addictive behaviors and a diminished ability to derive satisfaction from more meaningful and enduring activities. Additionally, the pressure to achieve instant results and the comparison with others' seemingly perfect lives on social media can contribute to feelings of inadequacy, anxiety, and depression. The expectation of immediate gratification can create a sense of impatience and frustration when things do not go as planned, leading to increased stress and a reduced capacity to cope with challenges.

Relationships are also affected by the instant gratification trap. The ease of digital communication has made it possible to connect with others instantly, but it has also led to a devaluation of face-to-face interactions and the development of meaningful relationships. The expectation of immediate responses and the tendency to seek quick validation can result in superficial interactions and a lack of deep, meaningful connections. This can lead to feelings of loneliness and isolation, as the quality of our relationships suffers in the pursuit of instant gratification. Furthermore, the ease of accessing entertainment and distractions online can reduce the time and effort we invest in nurturing our relationships, leading to a decline in the quality of our social interactions.

The instant gratification trap is not just a personal issue but a societal one as well. Our culture of immediacy, driven by consumerism and the pursuit of convenience, has created an environment where instant rewards are highly valued and patience is often overlooked. The constant bombardment of advertisements and messages promoting quick fixes and instant solutions reinforces the belief that satisfaction should be immediate and effort minimal. This cultural emphasis on speed and convenience can lead to a collective impatience and a reluctance to invest time and effort in long-term pursuits, such as education, career development, and personal growth.

To counteract the instant gratification trap, it is essential to cultivate patience and long-term thinking. Patience is the ability to endure delays and obstacles without becoming frustrated or disheartened. It involves maintaining a focus on long-term goals and the willingness to delay immediate rewards in favor of more significant, future benefits. Developing patience requires a shift in mindset and the adoption of strategies that promote self-discipline and resilience.

One effective strategy for developing patience is to practice mindfulness and self-awareness. Mindfulness involves being present in the moment and paying attention to our thoughts, feelings, and behaviors without judgment. By cultivating mindfulness, we can become more aware of our impulses and the triggers that lead to the pursuit of instant gratification. This awareness can help us to pause and reflect before acting, allowing us to make more deliberate and thoughtful choices that align with our long-term goals.

Another important strategy is to set clear, achievable goals and to break them down into smaller, manageable steps. By focusing on incremental progress and celebrating small successes along the way, we can maintain motivation and build momentum towards our larger objectives. This approach helps to shift our focus from immediate rewards to the satisfaction of making steady progress towards meaningful goals.

Developing self-discipline is also crucial for overcoming the instant gratification trap. Self-discipline involves the ability to control our impulses and to stay focused on our goals despite distractions and temptations. Techniques such as setting boundaries, creating routines, and practicing delayed gratification can help to strengthen self-discipline and reduce the tendency to seek immediate rewards. For example, setting specific times for checking social media or scheduling regular breaks during work can help to minimize distractions and maintain focus.

In addition to these individual strategies, it is also important to create an environment that supports patience and long-term thinking. This can involve reducing exposure to stimuli that promote instant gratification, such as limiting time spent on social media or avoiding advertisements that encourage impulsive buying. Creating a supportive social network that values and encourages long-term goals and personal growth can also help to reinforce positive behaviors and attitudes.

Education and awareness are also key to addressing the instant gratification trap at a societal level. Promoting the value of patience, perseverance, and delayed gratification through educational programs and public awareness campaigns can help to shift cultural attitudes and create a more supportive environment for long-term goal achievement. Encouraging critical thinking and media literacy can also help individuals to recognize and resist the messages that promote instant gratification and to make more informed and deliberate choices.

Chapter 31: Social Media and Creativity

Social media has profoundly transformed the way we create, share, and consume content, serving as both a catalyst for creativity and a breeding ground for imitation. Platforms like Instagram, TikTok, YouTube, and Pinterest have democratized creativity, allowing individuals from all walks of life to showcase their talents and reach global audiences. This unprecedented access to diverse creative expressions has sparked new waves of inspiration and innovation. However, it has also given rise to a culture of imitation, where trends can be quickly copied and originality sometimes gets overshadowed by the desire for virality and likes. The intricate relationship between social media and creativity involves a complex interplay of inspiration, imitation, collaboration, and competition, shaping the way we perceive and engage with creative works.

At its best, social media serves as an immense reservoir of inspiration. Users can discover new ideas, techniques, and perspectives from a virtually limitless pool of content. Artists, designers, musicians, writers, and other creatives share their work and processes, providing insight into their creative journeys. Platforms like Instagram and Pinterest are particularly rich in visual content, offering endless streams of images and videos that can spark new ideas. Similarly, TikTok and YouTube offer a wealth of tutorials, behind-the-scenes videos, and creative challenges that encourage users to experiment with new forms of expression.

This accessibility has led to the emergence of new creative communities and subcultures. For example, Instagram has given rise to the popularity of digital art and photography, while TikTok has become a hub for short-form video content and viral dance challenges. These platforms allow creatives to connect, collaborate, and build communities around shared interests and passions. Hashtags and user-generated content campaigns enable people to participate in global conversations, contributing their unique perspectives and expanding the collective creative landscape.

Moreover, social media has lowered the barriers to entry for aspiring creatives. Traditional gatekeepers, such as publishers, galleries, and record labels, are no longer the sole arbiters of success. Anyone with a smartphone and internet access can share their work and potentially reach millions of viewers. This democratization has led to the discovery of new talents and the proliferation of diverse voices that might have otherwise remained unheard. It has also fostered a sense of empowerment, as individuals can take control of their creative careers and build their own audiences.

However, the same features that make social media a powerful tool for inspiration also contribute to the prevalence of imitation. The algorithms that drive these platforms are designed to prioritize content that generates high engagement, often leading to the amplification of certain trends and styles. As users seek to replicate the success of viral content, they may be tempted to imitate popular formats, aesthetics, and themes rather than developing their own unique voices. This can result in a homogenization of content, where originality is sacrificed in favor of conformity and the pursuit of likes and followers.

Imitation is not inherently negative and can play a role in the learning process. For beginners, mimicking established styles and techniques can be a valuable way to develop skills and gain confidence. However, the pressure to conform to popular trends can stifle creativity and discourage risk-taking. Creatives may feel compelled to prioritize what is marketable over what is personally meaningful or innovative. This dynamic can create a challenging environment for those who strive to push boundaries and explore unconventional ideas.

The distinction between inspiration and imitation can be subtle and subjective. Drawing inspiration from others is a natural part of the creative process, and many groundbreaking works are the result of synthesizing influences from various sources. However, when imitation becomes mere replication without adding new value or perspective, it can undermine the originality and integrity of creative expression. The challenge for creatives is to navigate this fine line, finding ways to be inspired by others while maintaining their own unique vision and voice.

Social media's emphasis on metrics, such as likes, shares, and follower counts, can further complicate this landscape. The quantification of social approval can create external pressures that influence creative decisions. Creatives may feel incentivized to produce content that aligns with popular trends and garners immediate attention, rather than pursuing more experimental or personal projects that may not achieve the same level of instant validation. This can lead to a cycle where content becomes increasingly derivative and formulaic, as creators prioritize what is likely to perform well over what is truly original or innovative.

Despite these challenges, many creatives have found ways to leverage social media to foster genuine creativity and innovation. Some use the platform to document and share their creative processes, offering transparency and insight into the development of their work. This can demystify the creative process and provide valuable learning opportunities for others. Collaborative projects and user-generated content campaigns can also serve as powerful catalysts for creativity, as they encourage participants to build on each other's ideas and push the boundaries of their own work.

The interactive nature of social media can also enhance creativity by facilitating feedback and dialogue. Creatives can receive real-time input from their audiences, which can inform and refine their work. Engaging with a supportive community can provide motivation, encouragement, and constructive criticism, helping creators to grow and evolve. Additionally, social media can serve as a platform for experimenting with new formats and ideas, allowing creatives to test and iterate on their work in a dynamic and responsive environment.

The rise of influencers and content creators as new forms of celebrities has also reshaped the creative landscape. These individuals often blur the lines between inspiration and imitation, as they build their brands by curating and synthesizing trends, styles, and ideas from various sources. While some influencers are celebrated for their originality and innovation, others are criticized for perpetuating a culture of imitation and commodification. The influencer economy highlights the tension between creativity and commercialism, as creators navigate the pressures of maintaining authenticity while also achieving financial success and social validation.

To cultivate a healthy relationship with social media and creativity, it is important for individuals to be mindful of their motivations and intentions. Reflecting on why they create and what they hope to achieve can help creatives to stay true to their own visions and values. Setting boundaries around social media use and seeking out diverse sources of inspiration can also mitigate the risk of falling into the imitation trap. By prioritizing meaningful engagement over superficial metrics, creatives can foster deeper connections with their audiences and build more sustainable and fulfilling creative practices.

Educational institutions and creative organizations also have a role to play in addressing the challenges posed by social media. By promoting critical thinking, media literacy, and the importance of originality, they can equip individuals with the skills and perspectives needed to navigate the digital landscape. Encouraging collaboration, experimentation, and the exploration of diverse influences can help to counteract the homogenizing effects of social media and support the development of unique and innovative voices.

Chapter 32: The Power of Anonymity: Risks and Rewards

Anonymity has been a significant feature of human interaction, both in physical and virtual spaces, throughout history. The power of anonymity is a double-edged sword, offering a myriad of rewards and posing significant risks. In the digital age, anonymity plays a crucial role in shaping our online interactions, influencing the way we communicate, express ourselves, and engage with others. It allows individuals to explore their identities, share opinions freely, and protect their privacy. However, it also opens the door to malicious behaviors, misinformation, and a lack of accountability.

Anonymity, at its core, is the condition of being nameless or unidentifiable. In the online world, it allows individuals to interact without revealing their true identities, using pseudonyms or remaining entirely untraceable. This anonymity can provide a sense of freedom and safety, enabling people to express themselves more openly and honestly. One of the most significant rewards of anonymity is the ability to explore and express aspects of one's identity that might be suppressed in the offline world. For instance, individuals facing social stigmatization due to their sexual orientation, political beliefs, or personal interests can find solace and community in anonymous online spaces. These spaces provide a safe haven where they can be themselves without fear of judgment or retribution.

Anonymity also fosters creativity and innovation by removing the constraints of personal reputation and societal expectations. People can experiment with new ideas, engage in unconventional behaviors, and take risks that they might avoid if their real identities were known. This freedom can lead to the creation of unique and diverse content, from anonymous blogs and art to open-source software and collaborative projects. Platforms like Reddit and 4chan are known for their vibrant and sometimes controversial communities, where anonymity allows users to share ideas and creations that might not thrive in a more transparent environment.

In addition to personal expression and creativity, anonymity is crucial for protecting privacy and personal safety. Whistleblowers, activists, and journalists often rely on anonymity to expose corruption, injustice, and other sensitive issues without risking their careers, reputations, or lives. The ability to communicate anonymously can empower individuals to speak out against powerful entities and bring attention to important causes that might otherwise remain hidden. Anonymity can also protect ordinary individuals from various online threats, such as identity theft, harassment, and surveillance, by allowing them to control the information they share and maintain their privacy.

The concept of anonymity extends beyond individual benefits to societal and cultural impacts. Anonymity can contribute to a more open and democratic exchange of ideas by allowing people to participate in discussions and debates without fear of personal consequences. This can lead to a more diverse range of perspectives and a more inclusive dialogue, where marginalized voices have the opportunity to be heard. In some cases, anonymity can help to level the playing field, reducing the influence of social hierarchies and power dynamics that might otherwise dominate conversations.

However, the power of anonymity also comes with significant risks and challenges. One of the most concerning aspects is the potential for misuse and abuse. Anonymity can embolden individuals to engage in harmful behaviors that they would not exhibit if their identities were known. This includes cyberbullying, harassment, trolling, and the spread of hate speech and misinformation. The lack of accountability in anonymous spaces can lead to a toxic and hostile environment, where individuals feel free to act without regard for the consequences of their actions.

Cyberbullying, in particular, is a pervasive problem exacerbated by anonymity. The ability to harass or intimidate others without revealing one's identity can lead to severe psychological harm for victims, who may feel powerless to defend themselves or seek justice. Anonymity also complicates the efforts to combat online harassment, as perpetrators can easily evade detection and continue their harmful behaviors from behind the safety of their screens.

The spread of misinformation and fake news is another significant risk associated with anonymity. Anonymous sources can disseminate false or misleading information without fear of being held accountable, contributing to the erosion of trust in information and media. This can have far-reaching consequences, from influencing public opinion and election outcomes to inciting violence and undermining public health measures. The anonymity of content creators and sharers makes it difficult to trace the origins of misinformation and hold those responsible accountable for their actions.

Anonymity also presents challenges in maintaining security and preventing illegal activities. It can be exploited by individuals and groups engaged in criminal activities, such as hacking, fraud, and drug trafficking. The anonymity provided by the dark web, for example, has facilitated the growth of illegal marketplaces and forums where illicit goods and services are bought and sold with relative impunity. Law enforcement agencies face significant difficulties in tracking down and apprehending criminals operating under the cover of anonymity, complicating efforts to maintain public safety and security.

The use of anonymity in the context of online voting, surveys, and feedback mechanisms raises additional concerns. While anonymity can protect the privacy of participants and encourage honest responses, it also opens the door to manipulation and fraud. For instance, anonymous voting systems can be vulnerable to tampering and abuse, undermining the integrity of the democratic process. Similarly, anonymous feedback and review systems can be exploited for personal vendettas or to unfairly damage the reputation of individuals or businesses.

Balancing the rewards and risks of anonymity requires a nuanced approach that takes into account the context and purpose of its use. One of the key challenges is finding ways to protect the benefits of anonymity, such as privacy, freedom of expression, and creativity, while mitigating its potential for abuse. This involves developing and implementing policies, technologies, and practices that promote responsible use of anonymity and address its negative impacts.

One potential approach is to implement graduated levels of anonymity that vary depending on the context and potential risks involved. For example, platforms could require users to verify their identities for certain activities, such as financial transactions or participation in sensitive discussions, while allowing greater anonymity for less critical interactions, such as casual conversations or creative projects. This approach can help to balance the need for accountability and security with the desire for privacy and freedom of expression.

Another important strategy is to promote digital literacy and responsible online behavior. Educating individuals about the potential risks and responsibilities associated with anonymity can help to foster a more respectful and constructive online environment. Encouraging users to consider the impact of their actions and to adhere to community guidelines can reduce the prevalence of harmful behaviors, such as cyberbullying and harassment. Digital literacy programs can also help individuals to recognize and critically evaluate anonymous sources of information, reducing the spread of misinformation and promoting informed decision-making.

Technological solutions can also play a role in managing the risks of anonymity. Advanced algorithms and machine learning techniques can be used to detect and mitigate harmful behaviors, such as hate speech and misinformation, while preserving user privacy. For example, platforms can implement automated systems to flag and remove abusive content, or to identify patterns of behavior that indicate potential misuse of anonymity. These technologies can complement human moderation efforts, providing a more effective and scalable approach to maintaining a safe and respectful online environment.

Legal and regulatory frameworks are also essential for addressing the challenges of anonymity. Governments and international organizations can develop policies and regulations that promote transparency and accountability while protecting individuals' rights to privacy and freedom of expression. This can include measures to ensure that platforms have mechanisms in place for addressing abuse and illegal activities, such as reporting and removal procedures, and that they cooperate with law enforcement agencies when necessary. At the same time, it is important to safeguard against overreach and ensure that any measures taken to address the risks of anonymity do not unduly infringe on individuals' rights and freedoms.

Chapter 33: Building Community

The digital age has revolutionized the way we build communities and find like-minded individuals, often referred to as "finding your tribe." This concept of community building online goes beyond merely connecting with others; it encompasses the creation of meaningful relationships, shared experiences, and collective support systems. The process of finding and forming these virtual tribes has become an integral part of our social fabric, shaping how we interact, collaborate, and cultivate a sense of belonging in an increasingly interconnected world. The benefits of online communities are vast, ranging from emotional support and shared learning to collective action and cultural exchange. However, building and sustaining these communities also comes with challenges, such as managing conflicts, ensuring inclusivity, and navigating the complexities of digital communication.

The internet has provided an unparalleled platform for people to connect with others who share similar interests, values, and goals. Traditional geographical barriers that once limited community building have been dissolved, enabling individuals to find and engage with their tribes regardless of where they are located. This shift has made it possible for people to seek out and join communities that align with their passions, hobbies, and identities, fostering a sense of belonging that might not have been attainable in their immediate physical surroundings.

One of the most significant advantages of online communities is the ability to connect with people who share niche interests and specialized knowledge. For example, hobbyists in areas like vintage computing, rare book collecting, or obscure music genres can find dedicated communities that provide a wealth of information, resources, and camaraderie. Platforms such as Reddit, specialized forums, and social media groups allow individuals to exchange ideas, share expertise, and collaborate on projects with others who are equally passionate about their interests. This level of engagement can enhance personal fulfillment and contribute to the development of new skills and knowledge.

Moreover, online communities offer a unique space for individuals to explore and express aspects of their identity that might not be accepted or understood in their offline lives. For instance, Introverts, people with disabilities, or those with unconventional lifestyles can find support and validation in online groups that embrace and celebrate diversity. These communities provide a safe and affirming environment where members can share their experiences, seek advice, and form meaningful connections with others who understand their challenges and aspirations.

The emotional support provided by online communities is another crucial benefit. In times of personal crisis or when facing mental health struggles, individuals can turn to their virtual tribes for comfort, empathy, and guidance. Online support groups for people dealing with grief, addiction, or chronic illness, for example, offer a valuable source of connection and solidarity. These communities can provide a lifeline for those who feel isolated or stigmatized, offering a sense of belonging and reminding them that they are not alone in their experiences.

Beyond personal support and connection, online communities also play a vital role in facilitating collective action and social change. Activists and advocates can use digital platforms to mobilize support, raise awareness, and coordinate efforts to address social, political, and environmental issues. Movements such as #BlackLivesMatter, #MeToo, and climate activism have harnessed the power of online communities to amplify their messages and drive change on a global scale. By connecting individuals with shared values and goals, these communities can create a powerful force for positive impact and societal transformation.

Cultural exchange and global understanding are additional benefits of online communities. By connecting with people from different backgrounds, cultures, and perspectives, individuals can broaden their horizons and gain a deeper appreciation for the diversity of human experience. Online platforms provide opportunities for cross-cultural dialogue, collaborative learning, and the sharing of traditions and practices. This exchange can foster mutual respect and empathy, contributing to a more inclusive and interconnected world.

Despite the numerous advantages, building and maintaining online communities is not without its challenges. One of the primary difficulties is managing conflicts and disagreements within the community. Differences in opinions, values, and communication styles can lead to misunderstandings and tensions. Effective community management requires establishing clear guidelines for respectful interaction, fostering open and constructive dialogue, and addressing conflicts in a fair and transparent manner. This can help to create a positive and inclusive environment where all members feel valued and heard.

Ensuring inclusivity and accessibility is another critical aspect of successful online community building. It is essential to create spaces that welcome and support individuals from diverse backgrounds, including those with varying abilities, languages, and socioeconomic statuses. This may involve providing resources such as language translation, accessible content formats, and support for different communication preferences. By prioritizing inclusivity, communities can benefit from a wider range of perspectives and experiences, enriching the overall dialogue and fostering a more supportive and vibrant environment.

The dynamics of digital communication also present unique challenges for online communities. The lack of non-verbal cues and the potential for misinterpretation can make it difficult to convey tone and intent accurately. This can lead to misunderstandings and conflicts, as well as a sense of detachment or disconnection. To mitigate these challenges, it is important to encourage clear and thoughtful communication, provide context for interactions, and foster a culture of empathy and understanding. Utilizing multimedia tools, such as video and audio, can also help to bridge the gap between digital and face-to-face communication, enhancing the sense of connection and engagement among community members.

The rapid pace of digital interactions and the sheer volume of content can also pose challenges for community building. It can be difficult to keep up with the constant flow of information and to maintain meaningful connections amidst the noise. Community leaders and members must navigate the balance between staying informed and engaged while avoiding information overload and burnout. This may involve setting boundaries around online engagement, curating content to focus on relevant and meaningful topics, and fostering a culture of intentional and mindful interaction.

Sustaining online communities over time requires ongoing effort and commitment from both leaders and members. This involves nurturing a sense of shared purpose and belonging, encouraging active participation and contribution, and continuously adapting to the evolving needs and dynamics of the community. Regular events, discussions, and activities can help to maintain engagement and foster a sense of continuity and growth. Recognizing and celebrating the achievements and contributions of community members can also reinforce the value of the community and strengthen the bonds between individuals.

The role of technology in facilitating online communities is both a facilitator and a challenge. While digital platforms provide the tools and infrastructure for community building, they also shape the way we interact and engage with others. Algorithms, data privacy concerns, and the commercialization of digital spaces can impact the dynamics of online communities, influencing the content we see, the connections we make, and the overall culture of the community. It is important to critically assess the impact of these factors and to advocate for technologies and practices that prioritize the well-being and empowerment of community members.

Looking ahead, the future of online community building will likely continue to evolve with advances in technology and changes in social dynamics. Emerging technologies, such as virtual and augmented reality, have the potential to create even more immersive and interactive community experiences, blurring the lines between online and offline interactions. As our digital and physical lives become increasingly intertwined, the importance of fostering meaningful and supportive communities will remain a central aspect of our social fabric.

Chapter 34: The Economics of Attention

The economics of attention is a concept that has gained significant prominence in the digital age, particularly in the context of social media and the internet. It revolves around the idea that attention is a valuable resource that can be monetized. In a world where information is abundant, but human attention is finite, capturing and retaining attention has become a lucrative endeavor.

Attention is a finite resource. Unlike physical resources that can be produced or accumulated, human attention is limited by time and cognitive capacity. Every individual has only 24 hours in a day and can focus on a limited number of things at any given moment. This scarcity makes attention a highly sought-after commodity in the digital age, where an overwhelming amount of information competes for our limited cognitive resources.

The concept of attention economics is rooted in the notion that in the face of information overload, the most valuable thing is not the information itself, but the attention that information can attract. Herbert A. Simon, a Nobel laureate economist, succinctly captured this idea when he said, "A wealth of information creates a poverty of attention." In this context, businesses, advertisers, and content creators are all vying for the attention of consumers, which has become a critical factor in their success.

The rise of the internet and digital media has exponentially increased the amount of information available to individuals. This abundance of content has made it imperative for businesses to find ways to stand out and capture the attention of their target audience. Social media platforms, websites, mobile apps, and other digital channels have become the battlegrounds where attention is fought for, acquired, and monetized.

One of the primary ways in which attention is monetized is through advertising. Digital advertising has become a multi-billion-dollar industry, with companies willing to pay substantial amounts to place their ads in front of engaged audiences. Platforms like Google, Facebook, and YouTube have built their business models around capturing user attention and selling it to advertisers. These platforms offer sophisticated targeting capabilities, allowing advertisers to reach specific demographics, interests, and behaviors, thereby maximizing the effectiveness of their campaigns.

Google, for example, leverages its search engine to capture user attention by delivering relevant search results and ads. Every time a user performs a search, Google displays ads that are tailored to the user's query, interests, and previous interactions. Advertisers pay Google for these ad placements through a system known as pay-per-click (PPC), where they are charged each time, a user clicks on their ad. This model ensures that advertisers are only paying for actual engagement, making it a cost-effective way to capture attention.

Social media platforms like Facebook and Instagram use a similar approach. They offer advertisers the ability to create highly targeted ad campaigns based on user data such as age, gender, location, interests, and online behavior. These platforms also utilize sophisticated algorithms to deliver content that is most likely to engage users, thereby maximizing the amount of time users spend on the platform and the number of ads they are exposed to.

The attention economy is not limited to traditional advertising. Influencer marketing has emerged as a powerful strategy for monetizing attention. Influencers are individuals who have built substantial followings on social media platforms and are able to capture the attention of their audience through engaging content. Brands collaborate with influencers to promote their products or services, leveraging the trust and connection that influencers have established with their followers. This form of marketing can be highly effective, as it often feels more authentic and relatable than traditional advertising.

Another way attention is monetized is through content monetization strategies such as subscriptions, memberships, and premium content. Platforms like YouTube, Twitch, and Patreon allow content creators to earn money directly from their audience. On YouTube, creators can monetize their videos through ads, channel memberships, and Super Chat, where viewers pay to have their messages highlighted during live streams. Twitch, a platform primarily for live streaming, offers similar monetization options, including subscriptions, donations, and Bits, a virtual currency that viewers can purchase to support streamers.

Patreon takes a different approach by allowing creators to offer exclusive content to subscribers who pay a monthly fee. This model provides a steady stream of income for creators and allows them to build a community of dedicated supporters. It also incentivizes creators to consistently produce high-quality content that retains the attention of their subscribers.

The gaming industry also plays a significant role in the attention economy. Mobile games, in particular, have mastered the art of capturing and monetizing attention through a combination of free-to-play models and in-app purchases. Games like Candy Crush, Clash of Clans, and Fortnite are free to download and play, but they generate revenue by offering in-game items, enhancements, and currency that players can purchase. These games use a variety of techniques to keep players engaged, such as daily rewards, challenges, and social features that encourage competition and collaboration.

Attention monetization extends beyond entertainment and advertising into areas such as e-commerce and education. E-commerce platforms like Amazon use personalized recommendations and targeted ads to capture user attention and drive sales. By analyzing user behavior and preferences, these platforms can deliver highly relevant product suggestions that are more likely to result in purchases.

In the education sector, online learning platforms like Coursera, Udemy, and MasterClass monetize attention by offering courses and content that cater to the interests and needs of learners. These platforms use targeted marketing to attract students and keep them engaged through interactive content, quizzes, and community features.

The proliferation of smartphones and mobile apps has further intensified the competition for attention. Mobile apps use various techniques to capture and retain user attention, including push notifications, gamification, and personalized content. Push notifications, for example, serve as reminders and prompts that encourage users to return to the app. Gamification elements, such as badges, leaderboards, and rewards, create a sense of achievement and motivate users to stay engaged.

Personalization is a key strategy in the attention economy. By tailoring content, ads, and recommendations to individual preferences, businesses can increase the relevance and appeal of their offerings. This requires sophisticated data analytics and machine learning algorithms that analyze user behavior and predict what content or products are most likely to capture their attention. Personalization enhances user experience, fosters loyalty, and drives higher engagement rates.

However, the pursuit of attention monetization also raises ethical considerations. The techniques used to capture attention can sometimes lead to negative consequences, such as addiction, privacy concerns, and the spread of misinformation. Social media platforms, in particular, have been criticized for creating addictive experiences that prioritize engagement over user well-being. Features like infinite scrolling, autoplay videos, and algorithm-driven content feeds are designed to keep users hooked and spending more time on the platform.

Privacy is another significant concern. The collection and use of personal data to deliver targeted ads and personalized content raise questions about user consent and data security. High-profile data breaches and scandals, such as the Cambridge Analytica incident, have highlighted the risks associated with data-driven attention monetization.

Misinformation and fake news are also byproducts of the attention economy. In the race to capture attention, sensational and misleading content often performs better than factual information. This can lead to the spread of false narratives and the erosion of public trust in media and institutions. Platforms have a responsibility to address these issues and ensure that their practices align with ethical standards.

In response to these challenges, there is a growing movement towards more responsible and sustainable attention monetization. Companies are exploring ways to balance profitability with user well-being and ethical considerations. For example, some platforms are introducing features that allow users to set time limits, reduce distractions, and manage their digital consumption. There is also an increasing emphasis on transparency and user control over data privacy.

The future of attention economics will likely involve a continued evolution of strategies and technologies to capture and monetize attention. Artificial intelligence (AI) and machine learning will play a central role in refining personalization and targeting capabilities. Virtual reality (VR) and augmented reality (AR) are emerging technologies that offer immersive experiences, opening new avenues for attention capture and monetization.

Blockchain technology could also impact the attention economy by enabling more transparent and decentralized models of data sharing and monetization. For example, blockchain-based platforms could allow users to own and monetize their data directly, reducing the power imbalance between tech giants and individual users.

Chapter 35: Social Media Addiction: Recognizing the Signs

Social media addiction is a growing concern in today's digital age, characterized by an excessive, compulsive use of social media platforms that interferes with daily life, productivity, and personal well-being. As social media platforms have become integral to our personal and professional lives, recognizing the signs of addiction is crucial for maintaining a healthy balance and preventing negative consequences.

Social media addiction can be understood as a behavioral addiction where individuals become excessively preoccupied with social media to the detriment of other aspects of their lives. This condition shares similarities with other behavioral addictions, such as gambling addiction, in that it involves compulsive engagement in an activity despite its adverse effects. The constant need to check updates, post content, and interact with others online can create a cycle of dependency that is hard to break. One of the primary signs of social media addiction is the inability to control or reduce the use of social media. Individuals may find themselves spending more time on social media than intended, often at the expense of important activities like work, study, or personal relationships. Attempts to cut back on social media use may result in feelings of anxiety, irritability, or restlessness, which can drive individuals back to their devices.

Preoccupation with social media is another significant indicator. Addicted individuals may constantly think about social media, even when they are not using it. They might eagerly anticipate the next opportunity to check their feeds, post updates, or receive notifications. This preoccupation can lead to distraction and reduced attention to tasks at hand, negatively impacting productivity and performance. Another sign of social media addiction is the use of social media as a coping mechanism for negative emotions such as stress, loneliness, or depression. Just as some people turn to alcohol or drugs to escape from their problems, individuals addicted to social media may use it to numb or avoid their emotions. This reliance on social media for emotional relief can create a vicious cycle, where negative feelings drive increased use, which in turn exacerbates those feelings.

Social media addiction can also manifest in physical symptoms. Excessive use of digital devices can lead to eye strain, headaches, and sleep disturbances. The blue light emitted by screens interferes with the production of melatonin, a hormone that regulates sleep, leading to difficulties in falling asleep or poor quality sleep. Over time, these physical symptoms can contribute to chronic health problems, including insomnia and fatigue. Social isolation and a decline in face-to-face interactions are also common signs of social media addiction. While social media is designed to connect people, excessive use can have the opposite effect, leading to a preference for online interactions over real-life relationships. Individuals may withdraw from social activities, neglect personal relationships, and feel more comfortable communicating through screens than in person. This isolation can further exacerbate feelings of loneliness and depression.

The need for validation and approval is another hallmark of social media addiction. Individuals may become obsessed with the number of likes, comments, and shares their posts receive, viewing these metrics as indicators of their self-worth. This constant pursuit of online validation can lead to anxiety, low self-esteem, and a distorted sense of identity. People may also engage in behaviors aimed at increasing their social media popularity, such as posting provocative content or participating in viral trends, often compromising their values or privacy. The fear of missing out (FOMO) is closely linked to social media addiction. FOMO refers to the anxiety that arises from the perception that others are experiencing more enjoyable or fulfilling lives, as seen through their social media posts. This fear can drive individuals to compulsively check their feeds to stay updated and not miss out on any events, activities, or news. FOMO perpetuates the cycle of addiction, as individuals feel compelled to stay constantly connected to alleviate their anxiety.

Understanding the underlying causes of social media addiction is essential for addressing and mitigating its effects. Several factors contribute to the development of this addiction, including the design of social media platforms, psychological factors, and social influences. Social media platforms are designed to be addictive. They employ various psychological principles and techniques to capture and retain users' attention. Features such as infinite scrolling, notifications, likes, and algorithm-driven content feeds are all designed to create a sense of reward and anticipation. The intermittent reinforcement provided by these features, similar to the mechanics of slot machines, keeps users engaged and coming back for more.

Psychological factors also play a significant role in social media addiction. Individuals with low self-esteem, anxiety, depression, or other mental health issues may be more susceptible to developing an addiction. Social media can provide a temporary escape or a way to seek validation, making it particularly appealing to those struggling with negative emotions. Additionally, personality traits such as high levels of neuroticism or extraversion can increase vulnerability to social media addiction. Social influences and cultural norms also contribute to the prevalence of social media addiction. In today's society, being connected and active on social media is often seen as essential for social acceptance and professional success. Peer pressure, societal expectations, and the desire to fit in can drive individuals to engage excessively with social media, even when it negatively impacts their well-being.

The impact of social media addiction on mental health and well-being is profound. Studies have shown that excessive social media use is associated with increased levels of anxiety, depression, and loneliness. The constant exposure to idealized representations of others' lives can lead to feelings of inadequacy, jealousy, and low self-esteem. The pressure to present a perfect online persona can also contribute to stress and anxiety, as individuals strive to maintain a certain image and receive validation from others. Furthermore, social media addiction can negatively affect cognitive functioning. The constant distractions and interruptions from notifications and updates can impair attention, memory, and executive function. Multitasking between social media and other tasks reduces overall productivity and efficiency, leading to frustration and decreased performance in academic, professional, and personal endeavors.

The relationship between social media addiction and physical health is also significant. As mentioned earlier, excessive screen time can lead to eye strain, headaches, and sleep disturbances. The sedentary nature of social media use can contribute to a lack of physical activity, which is associated with various health problems, including obesity, cardiovascular disease, and musculoskeletal issues. Additionally, poor sleep quality resulting from late-night social media use can further exacerbate physical and mental health problems. Recognizing and addressing social media addiction requires a multifaceted approach that involves self-awareness, behavioral changes, and support from others. Here are some strategies to help mitigate the effects of social media addiction and promote a healthier relationship with digital technology:

The first step in addressing social media addiction is recognizing the problem. Individuals should take time to reflect on their social media usage patterns and assess how it impacts their daily lives, relationships, and well-being. Keeping a journal or using digital tools to track screen time can provide valuable insights into the extent of the addiction. Establishing clear boundaries around social media use is essential for managing addiction. This can include setting specific times for checking social media, limiting the duration of use, and creating tech-free zones or times, such as during meals or before bedtime. Using features like screen time limits and app blockers can help enforce these boundaries.

Practicing mindfulness in social media use involves being intentional and purposeful about how and why social media is used. This means avoiding mindless scrolling and focusing on meaningful interactions and content that adds value to one's life. Mindfulness techniques, such as meditation and deep breathing, can also help manage cravings and reduce stress. Finding and engaging in activities that do not involve screens can help reduce dependency on social media. This can include hobbies, physical exercise, spending time with loved ones, reading, and other fulfilling activities. Developing a diverse range of interests and activities can provide alternative sources of satisfaction and enjoyment. Addressing social media addiction can be challenging, and seeking support from friends, family, or professionals can be beneficial. Talking to a therapist or counselor can provide guidance and strategies for managing addiction and addressing underlying mental health issues. Support groups and online communities focused on digital detox and mindful technology use can also offer encouragement and accountability.

Periodically taking breaks from social media, known as digital detox, can help reset habits and reduce dependency. This can involve taking short breaks, such as a weekend off, or longer hiatuses, such as a month-long detox. During this time, individuals can focus on reconnecting with themselves and their surroundings without the constant distraction of social media. Individuals should periodically reevaluate their relationship with social media and consider whether it aligns with their values and goals. This may involve unfollowing accounts that negatively impact mental health, curating a more positive and inspiring feed, and being selective about the platforms and content consumed.

Encouraging digital well-being involves advocating for responsible and mindful use of technology at a societal level. This includes supporting policies and initiatives that promote digital literacy, mental health awareness, and ethical technology design. Educating others about the signs of social media addiction and strategies for healthy use can also contribute to a more balanced and mindful digital culture.

Chapter 36: Navigating Negativity

Navigating negativity and handling online criticism has become a vital skill in the digital age, where individuals are frequently exposed to a myriad of opinions, both positive and negative, on social media platforms, forums, and other online spaces. The internet's anonymity can embolden people to express their thoughts in harsh and unfiltered ways, making the experience of receiving criticism particularly challenging.

Online criticism can range from constructive feedback aimed at helping someone improve to outright bullying and harassment. Constructive criticism is typically specific, actionable, and delivered with the intent of fostering growth. For instance, a comment suggesting ways to enhance a project or improve a skill can be valuable and contribute to personal development. However, the anonymity and impersonal nature of the internet often lead to destructive criticism, which can be vague, overly harsh, or even personal attacks designed to hurt the recipient.

The psychological impact of online criticism can be profound, particularly when it crosses the line into cyberbullying or trolling. Negative comments can trigger feelings of inadequacy, anxiety, and depression, especially if the individual is already vulnerable or experiencing low self-esteem. The phenomenon of "negativity bias," where people tend to focus more on negative experiences than positive ones, can exacerbate the impact of online criticism. Even a single harsh comment can overshadow numerous positive interactions, leading to a distorted perception of oneself and one's abilities.

Moreover, the persistence and public nature of online criticism can amplify its effects. Unlike face-to-face interactions, where negative feedback might be limited to a small audience and a fleeting moment, online criticism can be seen by a vast number of people and remain accessible indefinitely. This can intensify feelings of humiliation and helplessness, as the criticism becomes part of one's digital footprint, potentially impacting personal and professional opportunities.

To navigate negativity and handle online criticism effectively, it is essential to develop a balanced perspective and employ practical strategies. The first step in managing online criticism is to differentiate between constructive feedback and destructive criticism. Constructive feedback, even if difficult to hear, can offer valuable insights and opportunities for growth. Embracing such feedback involves setting aside emotional reactions and focusing on the content of the criticism. Asking oneself questions like "Is there any truth to this feedback?" or "How can I use this information to improve?" can help transform potentially negative experiences into positive learning moments.

On the other hand, destructive criticism should be approached with caution. It is important to recognize that not all criticism is valid or worth considering. Destructive criticism often reflects the critic's issues rather than the recipient's flaws. Adopting a mindset of critical thinking can help in evaluating the source and intent of the criticism. Questions such as "Does this person have expertise or authority on this subject?" and "Is this feedback specific and actionable?" can aid in filtering out unhelpful comments.

Another crucial aspect of handling online criticism is maintaining emotional resilience. Developing resilience involves building a strong sense of self-worth that is not easily shaken by external opinions. This can be achieved through self-reflection, self-compassion, and focusing on one's strengths and achievements. Practicing mindfulness and stress-reduction techniques, such as meditation and deep breathing, can also help in managing emotional reactions to negative feedback.

Setting boundaries is a vital strategy for managing online criticism. This includes deciding when and how to engage with online platforms. Taking regular breaks from social media, limiting exposure to potentially toxic environments, and curating one's online experience by following positive and supportive accounts can reduce the likelihood of encountering excessive negativity. Utilizing privacy settings and blocking or muting individuals who consistently provide harmful feedback can create a safer and more positive online environment.

Engaging in healthy communication and conflict resolution is another effective approach. When responding to online criticism, it is essential to remain calm and composed. Reacting impulsively or defensively can escalate the situation and lead to further negativity. Instead, taking time to reflect on the feedback and crafting a thoughtful response can help in addressing the criticism constructively. Acknowledging valid points, expressing appreciation for constructive feedback, and clarifying misunderstandings can turn a potentially negative interaction into a productive dialogue.

Seeking support from trusted friends, family, or professional counselors can also be beneficial. Sharing experiences and feelings with others can provide emotional relief and different perspectives on handling criticism. Online support groups and communities can offer solidarity and practical advice from individuals who have faced similar challenges. Professional counseling or therapy can provide tools and strategies for building resilience and managing the emotional impact of online criticism.

Creating a healthier online environment requires collective efforts from individuals, communities, and platforms. Individuals can contribute by promoting positive interactions and being mindful of their online behavior. Practicing digital empathy, which involves understanding and considering the emotions and experiences of others, can foster a more compassionate and supportive online culture. Communities can establish norms and guidelines that encourage respectful communication and discourage harmful behavior. Moderators and administrators play a crucial role in enforcing these standards and ensuring a safe space for all members.

Social media platforms and online forums also have a responsibility to address the issue of online criticism and negativity. Implementing features such as reporting mechanisms, content moderation, and algorithms that detect and mitigate harmful behavior can help in reducing the prevalence of destructive criticism. Platforms can also promote digital literacy and awareness campaigns that educate users about the impact of their words and the importance of constructive feedback.

Educational institutions and organizations can play a pivotal role in equipping individuals with the skills to handle online criticism. Incorporating digital literacy and emotional intelligence training into curricula can help students navigate the complexities of online interactions. Workshops and seminars on resilience, stress management, and conflict resolution can empower individuals to manage criticism effectively and maintain their well-being.

Chapter 37: From Likes to Love: Social Media and Dating

The advent of social media has revolutionized many aspects of our lives, including how we form and maintain romantic relationships. From the initial stages of attraction and flirting to the complex dynamics of long-term relationships, social media has become an integral part of modern dating.

Social media has fundamentally altered the way people meet and connect. Traditionally, people met potential partners through mutual acquaintances, social gatherings, or workplace interactions. While these avenues still exist, social media has expanded the possibilities by allowing individuals to connect with a much broader pool of potential partners. Platforms like Facebook, Instagram, and Twitter provide a space where people can present themselves, explore others' profiles, and initiate contact based on shared interests and mutual connections. Dating apps such as Tinder, Bumble, and Hinge have taken this a step further by explicitly focusing on romantic connections, making it easier than ever to find potential matches.

One of the primary ways social media impacts dating is through the creation of a curated online persona. Individuals often present an idealized version of themselves on social media, showcasing their best moments, achievements, and physical appearances. This curation can influence initial attraction, as people tend to be drawn to profiles that project confidence, success, and attractiveness. However, this idealization can also lead to unrealistic expectations and disappointment when real-life interactions do not align with the online persona. The phenomenon of "catfishing," where individuals create fake profiles to deceive others, is an extreme example of how online representations can be misleading.

The initial stages of romantic interest and flirting have also been transformed by social media. Liking, commenting, and sharing content are now common ways to signal interest and initiate interaction. These digital gestures can serve as a modern form of courtship, allowing individuals to express attraction and engage in playful banter. The use of direct messaging (DMs) provides a private channel for more intimate conversations, making it easier to establish a connection without the pressure of face-to-face interactions. Emojis, gifs, and memes add a layer of nuance and humor to digital flirting, enabling individuals to convey emotions and intentions in creative ways.

Social media facilitates continuous communication and interaction, which is crucial for relationship development. Couples can stay connected throughout the day by sharing updates, photos, and messages, fostering a sense of closeness and intimacy. This constant connectivity can be particularly beneficial for long-distance relationships, as it allows partners to maintain regular contact and share experiences despite physical separation. Video calls, live streaming, and social media stories provide additional ways for couples to feel present in each other's lives, enhancing the sense of togetherness.

However, the omnipresence of social media in dating also presents several challenges. One significant issue is the potential for miscommunication and misunderstanding. The lack of non-verbal cues and the brevity of digital communication can lead to misinterpretations of tone and intent. For example, a message intended to be lighthearted and humorous might be perceived as sarcastic or dismissive, leading to unnecessary conflicts. Additionally, the public nature of social media interactions can create complications. Likes, comments, and interactions with other users can trigger jealousy and insecurity, particularly if one partner perceives these actions as flirtatious or inappropriate. The visibility of past relationships and interactions can also be a source of tension, as it may lead to comparisons and doubts about the current relationship's status and significance.

Privacy concerns are another critical issue in the context of social media and dating. Sharing personal information, photos, and intimate details online can expose individuals to risks such as identity theft, stalking, and harassment. It is essential for individuals to be mindful of their privacy settings and to consider the potential consequences of sharing certain information online. Trust and mutual respect are crucial in navigating these privacy concerns within a relationship. Partners need to communicate openly about their boundaries and expectations regarding social media use to ensure that both feel comfortable and secure.

The phenomenon of "relationship visibility" on social media, where couples publicly display their relationship status and share moments from their lives together, has both positive and negative implications. On the positive side, sharing relationship milestones and affectionate posts can reinforce the bond between partners and provide a sense of validation and support from their social network. Public displays of affection (PDA) on social media can also signal commitment and exclusivity, helping to strengthen the relationship.

However, the pressure to maintain a perfect online image can be detrimental. The constant comparison to other couples' seemingly idyllic lives can create unrealistic expectations and dissatisfaction. The desire to present a flawless relationship can lead to the suppression of genuine issues and emotions, resulting in a lack of authenticity and vulnerability. Moreover, the end of a relationship can be particularly challenging to navigate on social media. The process of "uncoupling" online, such as changing relationship statuses, deleting photos, and unfollowing or blocking an ex-partner, can be painful and complicated. The visibility of an ex-partner's life post-breakup can hinder the healing process and prolong emotional distress.

Social media also plays a role in the dynamics of relationship maintenance and conflict resolution. The ease of communication can be both a blessing and a curse. On one hand, it allows couples to quickly address issues and stay connected; on the other hand, it can facilitate impulsive reactions and escalation of conflicts. The temptation to vent frustrations publicly or seek validation from others during a conflict can undermine the relationship and exacerbate tensions. Constructive conflict resolution requires open and respectful communication, which can be challenging to achieve through digital means alone.

Balancing social media use with real-life interactions is essential for healthy relationship development. While social media can enhance communication and connectivity, it should not replace face-to-face interactions and genuine emotional intimacy. Setting boundaries around social media use, such as designated "tech-free" times or activities, can help couples prioritize quality time together and strengthen their bond. Being present and fully engaged during in-person interactions is crucial for building trust and deepening the connection.

The influence of social media on dating extends beyond individual relationships to broader societal trends and cultural norms. Social media has contributed to the rise of online dating culture, where meeting potential partners through digital platforms is increasingly normalized and accepted. This shift has democratized dating, making it more accessible and inclusive for people from diverse backgrounds and communities. However, it has also introduced new complexities and challenges, such as the prevalence of ghosting (sudden and unexplained cessation of communication) and the pressure to present oneself in a certain way to attract matches.

The concept of "relationship goals," popularized on social media, reflects idealized portrayals of romantic relationships that can influence individuals' perceptions and expectations. While these portrayals can be inspiring and aspirational, they can also create pressure to conform to unrealistic standards and undermine genuine self-expression. It is important for individuals to critically assess the content they consume and recognize the difference between curated online representations and real-life relationships.

Chapter 38: Future of Social Media: Trends to Watch

The future of social media promises to be dynamic and transformative, driven by technological advancements, evolving user behaviors, and emerging societal needs. As platforms continue to innovate and adapt, several key trends are poised to shape the landscape of social media.

One of the most significant trends shaping the future of social media is the rise of augmented reality (AR) and virtual reality (VR). These technologies are set to revolutionize how users interact with digital content and each other. Augmented reality, which overlays digital information onto the physical world, is already being used in filters and interactive experiences on platforms like Instagram and Snapchat. As AR technology becomes more sophisticated, we can expect more immersive and interactive content that blurs the line between the digital and physical realms. Virtual reality, on the other hand, offers fully immersive experiences in digital environments. Social media platforms are beginning to explore VR's potential to create virtual spaces where users can meet, socialize, and engage in activities together. This could lead to the development of virtual social networks, where users create avatars and interact in 3D environments, transforming the way we experience social interactions online.

Another major trend is the increasing integration of artificial intelligence (AI) and machine learning into social media platforms. AI is already being used to personalize content feeds, recommend friends, and target advertisements. In the future, AI's role is likely to expand, enabling more sophisticated content curation and user engagement strategies. For instance, AI could be used to create highly personalized content recommendations based on user behavior, preferences, and interests. Additionally, AI-driven chatbots and virtual assistants could enhance customer service and engagement on social media, providing instant support and interaction. Machine learning algorithms could also be employed to detect and mitigate harmful content, such as misinformation, hate speech, and cyberbullying, creating a safer online environment.

The rise of short-form video content is another trend that is set to dominate the future of social media. Platforms like TikTok have popularized the format, prompting other social media giants like Instagram (with Reels) and YouTube (with Shorts) to follow suit. The appeal of short-form videos lies in their ability to capture attention quickly and convey messages concisely. As users' attention spans continue to shorten, the demand for bite-sized, engaging content will grow. This trend will likely lead to an increase in user-generated content, as more people embrace the simplicity and accessibility of creating short videos. Brands and marketers will also need to adapt their strategies to leverage this format, focusing on creativity and authenticity to capture audience attention.

Social commerce is another burgeoning trend that will shape the future of social media. The integration of e-commerce features directly into social media platforms has already begun, with Instagram Shopping, Facebook Marketplace, and TikTok's shopping features leading the way. This trend is set to expand, transforming social media into a primary channel for online shopping. Social commerce offers a seamless shopping experience, allowing users to discover, research, and purchase products without leaving the platform. Influencer marketing will play a significant role in this space, as influencers can drive product discovery and influence purchasing decisions through authentic endorsements and reviews. Augmented reality will further enhance social commerce by enabling virtual try-ons and immersive shopping experiences, allowing users to visualize products in their environment before making a purchase.

The future of social media will also see a greater emphasis on privacy and data security. In response to growing concerns about data breaches, surveillance, and misuse of personal information, users are demanding more control over their data and privacy settings. Social media platforms will need to prioritize user privacy by implementing robust data protection measures and offering transparent privacy policies. Decentralized social networks, which are built on blockchain technology and offer greater user control and privacy, may gain traction as users seek alternatives to traditional platforms. These networks operate without a central authority, giving users more control over their data and content, and potentially transforming the power dynamics of social media.

The concept of digital well-being is another trend that will influence the future of social media. As awareness of the potential negative impacts of social media on mental health grows, platforms will need to take proactive steps to promote digital well-being. This could include features that encourage healthy usage habits, such as time management tools, reminders to take breaks, and customizable notification settings. Platforms may also invest in content that promotes positivity, mental health resources, and community support initiatives. The integration of AI-driven tools that can detect signs of distress and offer support or intervention could further enhance digital well-being on social media.

Another significant trend is the evolution of content moderation practices. The spread of misinformation, hate speech, and harmful content has highlighted the need for effective content moderation on social media platforms. Future content moderation will likely involve a combination of AI and human oversight to ensure accuracy and fairness. Platforms will need to develop more sophisticated algorithms to detect and remove harmful content while minimizing false positives. Transparency in moderation practices and clear communication with users about why certain content is removed or flagged will be essential in building trust and maintaining a positive user experience.

The emergence of new social media platforms and the diversification of existing ones will also characterize the future landscape. As user preferences and behaviors evolve, there will be opportunities for new platforms to cater to niche audiences and specific interests. For example, platforms focused on audio content, such as Clubhouse and Twitter Spaces, have gained popularity, tapping into the growing demand for audio-based social interactions. These platforms provide spaces for live conversations, discussions, and events, offering a different kind of social experience compared to traditional text and video-based platforms.

The integration of social media with other technologies and industries will further expand its influence and applications. For instance, the convergence of social media and gaming is creating new opportunities for social interactions within virtual worlds. Platforms like Twitch and Discord are blurring the lines between gaming and social networking, providing spaces for gamers to connect, share content, and build communities. The use of social media in education, healthcare, and professional networking will also continue to grow, offering new ways to connect, share knowledge, and collaborate.

The role of influencers and content creators will continue to evolve in the future of social media. As the influencer economy matures, there will be greater emphasis on authenticity, niche expertise, and long-term partnerships. Micro-influencers, who have smaller but highly engaged audiences, will play a significant role in this space, offering more personalized and relatable content. The rise of subscription-based models, such as Patreon and OnlyFans, will provide new monetization opportunities for content creators, allowing them to build sustainable income streams from their most dedicated followers.

Chapter 39: Balancing Act

Balancing the integration of social media into one's life is an increasingly complex challenge in our hyper-connected world. As social media platforms become more ingrained in our daily routines, finding a healthy equilibrium between online and offline activities is crucial for maintaining mental well-being, fostering genuine relationships, and ensuring productivity.

Social media platforms like Facebook, Instagram, Twitter, and TikTok have transformed how we communicate, socialize, and access information. They offer numerous benefits, including the ability to stay connected with friends and family, share experiences, and discover new interests. Social media has also democratized information, providing a platform for voices that might otherwise be marginalized. It has fostered global communities, enabling people with shared interests or causes to come together and mobilize for change. For businesses and professionals, social media offers powerful tools for marketing, networking, and brand building.

Despite these advantages, excessive social media use can lead to a range of negative consequences. One of the most significant concerns is its impact on mental health. Studies have linked heavy social media use to increased feelings of anxiety, depression, and loneliness. The constant comparison with others' curated lives can lead to feelings of inadequacy and low self-esteem. The phenomenon known as FOMO (fear of missing out) can exacerbate these feelings, as individuals worry that they are not experiencing life as fully as their peers.

Another concern is the effect of social media on attention and productivity. The design of social media platforms encourages constant engagement, with notifications, likes, and comments creating a cycle of reward that can be difficult to break. This can lead to frequent interruptions, reducing the ability to focus on tasks and diminishing overall productivity. The compulsive checking of social media can also encroach on time that could be spent on more meaningful activities, such as hobbies, exercise, or face-to-face interactions.

Social media can also impact real-life relationships. While it provides a convenient way to stay in touch, it can also create a false sense of connection. Online interactions often lack the depth and authenticity of in-person communication. Over-reliance on social media for socializing can lead to weakened interpersonal skills and a reduced ability to form and maintain meaningful relationships. Additionally, the public nature of social media can lead to conflicts and misunderstandings, as personal issues and disagreements play out in a visible arena.

To achieve a balanced integration of social media into one's life, it is essential to develop mindful and intentional usage habits. The first step is to become aware of one's social media habits and their impact. This involves reflecting on how much time is spent on social media, the emotions experienced during and after use, and the ways in which it affects other areas of life. Keeping a journal or using tracking apps can help in gaining insights into usage patterns and identifying areas that need adjustment.

Setting clear boundaries around social media use is crucial for maintaining balance. This can include designating specific times for checking social media, such as during breaks or after work, and avoiding its use during certain activities, such as meals, family time, or before bedtime. Creating a structured routine that prioritizes offline activities can help in reducing the impulse to check social media constantly. For instance, scheduling regular exercise, hobbies, and social interactions can provide fulfilling alternatives to scrolling through feeds.

It is also important to curate one's social media environment to enhance positive experiences and minimize negative ones. This involves being selective about whom to follow and what content to engage with. Following accounts that inspire, educate, or uplift can create a more positive social media experience. Conversely, unfollowing or muting accounts that cause stress, anxiety, or negative self-comparison can help in reducing exposure to harmful content. Engaging in digital decluttering, where unnecessary or unwanted connections and content are regularly removed, can also contribute to a healthier online environment.

Practicing digital detoxes can be an effective strategy for recalibrating one's relationship with social media. This involves taking intentional breaks from social media for a set period, such as a weekend, a week, or even longer. Digital detoxes can help in breaking the cycle of compulsive checking, reducing dependency, and gaining perspective on the role of social media in one's life. During these breaks, individuals can focus on offline activities that promote well-being, such as spending time in nature, reading, or engaging in creative pursuits.

Building digital literacy and critical thinking skills is essential for navigating the complexities of social media. This involves understanding how social media platforms operate, including their algorithms, data collection practices, and the ways in which they shape content visibility and user engagement. Being aware of these factors can help users make more informed decisions about their social media use and reduce susceptibility to manipulation. Critical thinking also involves questioning the authenticity of online content, recognizing bias, and avoiding the spread of misinformation.

Engaging in meaningful interactions and fostering genuine connections on social media can enhance its positive aspects. Instead of passively consuming content, actively participating in discussions, sharing thoughtful comments, and connecting with others on a deeper level can create a more fulfilling social media experience. Joining online communities that align with one's interests and values can also provide a sense of belonging and support.

Balancing social media use also requires addressing its impact on sleep and physical health. Excessive screen time, particularly before bedtime, can interfere with sleep quality and disrupt circadian rhythms. Establishing a digital curfew, where screens are turned off at least an hour before bed, can help in promoting better sleep. Incorporating physical activities into daily routines, such as regular exercise and outdoor time, can counteract the sedentary nature of social media use and improve overall health.

For parents and caregivers, guiding children and adolescents in their social media use is crucial. This involves setting age-appropriate boundaries, monitoring online activities, and fostering open communication about the benefits and risks of social media. Encouraging healthy habits, such as balancing screen time with offline activities, promoting digital literacy, and teaching respectful online behavior, can help young people develop a balanced relationship with social media.

Organizations and employers also have a role to play in promoting balanced social media use. This can include creating policies that encourage mindful social media practices, such as limiting personal social media use during work hours and providing resources for digital well-being. Offering training and support for managing digital stress and promoting a healthy work-life balance can contribute to overall employee well-being and productivity.

The future of social media will likely bring new challenges and opportunities for achieving balance. Emerging technologies, such as augmented reality, virtual reality, and artificial intelligence, will continue to transform the social media landscape. Staying informed about these developments and their potential impact can help individuals adapt their usage habits and maintain a healthy balance.

Chapter 40: Conclusion: Living Beyond the Screen

Living beyond the screen encompasses the journey of reclaiming real-life experiences and human connections in an era dominated by digital interactions. As screens become ever more integral to our daily routines—through smartphones, computers, and other digital devices—our lives increasingly unfold in virtual spaces. This profound shift necessitates a conscious effort to cultivate a life that transcends the digital realm, fostering a richer, more fulfilling existence that prioritizes tangible experiences, face-to-face interactions, and personal well-being.

The ubiquitous presence of screens has fundamentally altered how we interact with the world. Digital devices provide unparalleled convenience and connectivity, enabling us to communicate instantly, access vast information, and entertain ourselves with a few taps. However, the convenience of digital life comes with a cost. Excessive screen time is linked to a range of negative outcomes, including diminished attention spans, increased stress levels, and a sense of disconnection from the physical world. Research indicates that the blue light emitted by screens can disrupt sleep patterns, while the constant influx of notifications and digital stimuli can lead to information overload and cognitive fatigue. Recognizing these consequences is the first step towards finding a balance that allows us to enjoy the benefits of technology without being overwhelmed by it.

Living beyond the screen means making a deliberate effort to disconnect from digital devices and engage more fully with the present moment. This involves practicing mindfulness, a mental state achieved by focusing one's awareness on the present, often through meditation or other contemplative practices. Mindfulness helps individuals become more attuned to their surroundings, thoughts, and feelings, reducing the automatic urge to reach for a device when faced with idle moments. By cultivating mindfulness, people can develop a greater appreciation for the world around them, enhancing their sensory experiences and deepening their emotional responses.

A crucial aspect of living beyond the screen is fostering face-to-face relationships. Digital communication, while convenient, often lacks the depth and nuance of in-person interactions. Non-verbal cues such as body language, facial expressions, and tone of voice play a significant role in human communication, helping to convey empathy, understanding, and emotional support. In-person interactions allow for these subtleties to be fully expressed, leading to more meaningful and satisfying relationships. Spending quality time with loved ones, engaging in shared activities, and participating in community events can strengthen social bonds and create lasting memories that digital interactions cannot replicate.

Another important dimension of living beyond the screen is the pursuit of physical activities. Regular exercise is essential for maintaining physical health, reducing stress, and boosting mental well-being. Physical activities can range from structured workouts at the gym to outdoor pursuits such as hiking, cycling, or gardening. Engaging in physical activities not only benefits the body but also provides a break from screens, offering an opportunity to connect with nature and experience the world in a more embodied way. For many, outdoor activities provide a sense of adventure and exploration, fostering a connection with the natural environment and promoting a sense of wonder and curiosity.

Creativity and personal growth are also key components of a life beyond the screen. The digital world offers endless content for consumption, but true fulfillment often comes from creation rather than consumption. Pursuing creative endeavors such as writing, painting, playing music, or crafting allows individuals to express themselves, develop new skills, and experience the satisfaction of making something tangible. These activities provide a sense of purpose and achievement that passive consumption of digital content cannot offer. Additionally, engaging in creative pursuits can be a form of self-care, offering a therapeutic outlet for emotions and a means of exploring one's inner world.

Living beyond the screen also involves reevaluating our relationship with time. The fast-paced nature of the digital world can create a sense of urgency and impatience, leading us to prioritize speed over quality. By slowing down and embracing a more deliberate approach to life, we can savor experiences more fully and appreciate the small moments that often go unnoticed. This might involve practicing "slow living" principles, such as cooking meals from scratch, enjoying leisurely walks, or dedicating time to hobbies and interests without the distraction of digital devices. Slowing down allows us to reconnect with our intrinsic rhythms and live more in harmony with our natural pace.

Education and personal development are areas where living beyond the screen can have a profound impact. While online courses and digital learning resources offer convenience and accessibility, there is immense value in experiential learning and hands-on experiences. Participating in workshops, attending lectures, and engaging in collaborative projects can deepen our understanding and foster a sense of community and shared purpose. Learning in a physical environment allows for spontaneous interactions and real-time feedback, enriching the educational experience and promoting a deeper connection to the subject matter.

Cultivating digital boundaries is another essential strategy for living beyond the screen. This involves setting limits on screen time, creating device-free zones and times, and prioritizing offline activities. For instance, implementing a "no screens at the dinner table" rule can encourage family members to engage in meaningful conversations and strengthen familial bonds. Similarly, designating certain hours of the day as "tech-free" can help create space for reflection, relaxation, and personal connection. Establishing these boundaries requires discipline and a conscious effort to resist the lure of digital devices, but the benefits for mental health and overall well-being are substantial.

Community engagement and social responsibility are also important aspects of a balanced life. Volunteering, participating in local events, and supporting community initiatives can provide a sense of purpose and belonging. These activities offer opportunities to meet new people, develop empathy, and contribute to the greater good. Engaging in community service can also help shift our focus from the virtual world to the real world, reminding us of the tangible impact we can have on others' lives.

Finally, living beyond the screen means embracing the concept of digital minimalism. This philosophy advocates for a more intentional and mindful use of technology, focusing on quality over quantity. Digital minimalism encourages individuals to critically assess their digital habits and eliminate unnecessary distractions, allowing for a more focused and meaningful engagement with technology. By adopting this mindset, we can reduce digital clutter, prioritize essential tasks, and create space for activities that enrich our lives.

The End.